LAKE TITICACA: LEGEND, MYTH, & SCIENCE

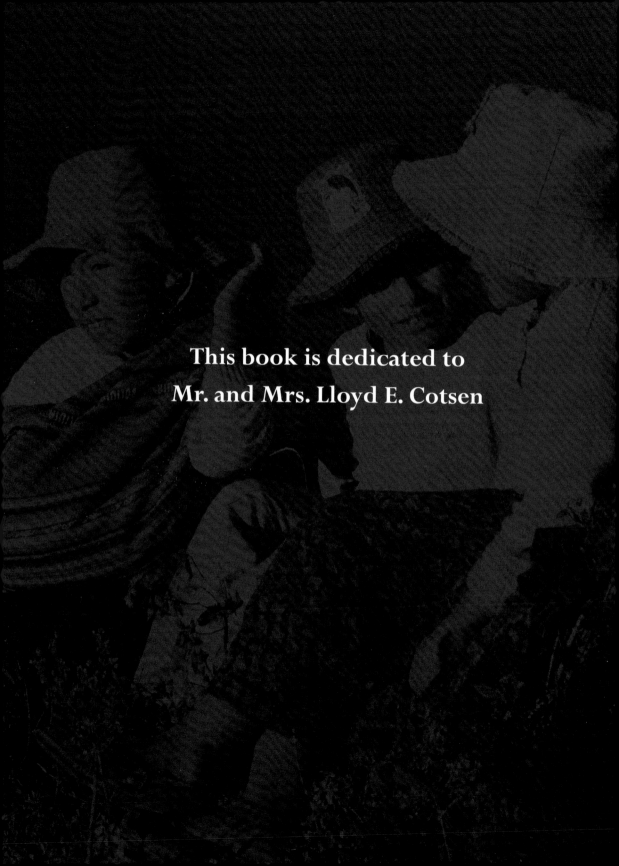

This book is dedicated to
Mr. and Mrs. Lloyd E. Cotsen

Lake Titicaca

Legend, Myth and Science

Charles Stanish
Cotsen Institute of Archaeology
University of California, Los Angeles

This book is set in 12-point Perpetua Text.
Edited by Peg Goldstein
Designed by Matt Pfingsten, Eric Gardner & Abishek Goel

Library of Congress Cataloging-in-Publication Data
Stanish, Charles, 1956-
  Lake Titicaca : legend, myth and science / Charles Stanish.
     p. cm. -- (World heritage and monument series ; v. 2)
  Includes bibliographical references and index.
  ISBN 978-1-931745-82-6 (pbk.)
1. Aymara Indians--Titicaca, Lake, Region (Peru and Bolivia) 2. Aymara mythology--Titicaca, Lake, Region (Peru and Bolivia) 3. Quechua Indians--Titicaca, Lake, Region (Peru and Bolivia) 4. Quechua mythology--Titicaca, Lake, Region (Peru and Bolivia) 5. Legends--Titicaca, Lake, Region (Peru and Bolivia) 6. Titicaca, Lake, Region (Peru and Bolivia)--Folklore. 7. Titicaca, Lake, Region (Peru and Bolivia)--Antiquities. 8. Titicaca, Lake, Region (Peru and Bolivia)--Description and travel. I. Title.
  F2230.2.A9S73 2011
  984'.12--dc22
                                2011016492

Contents

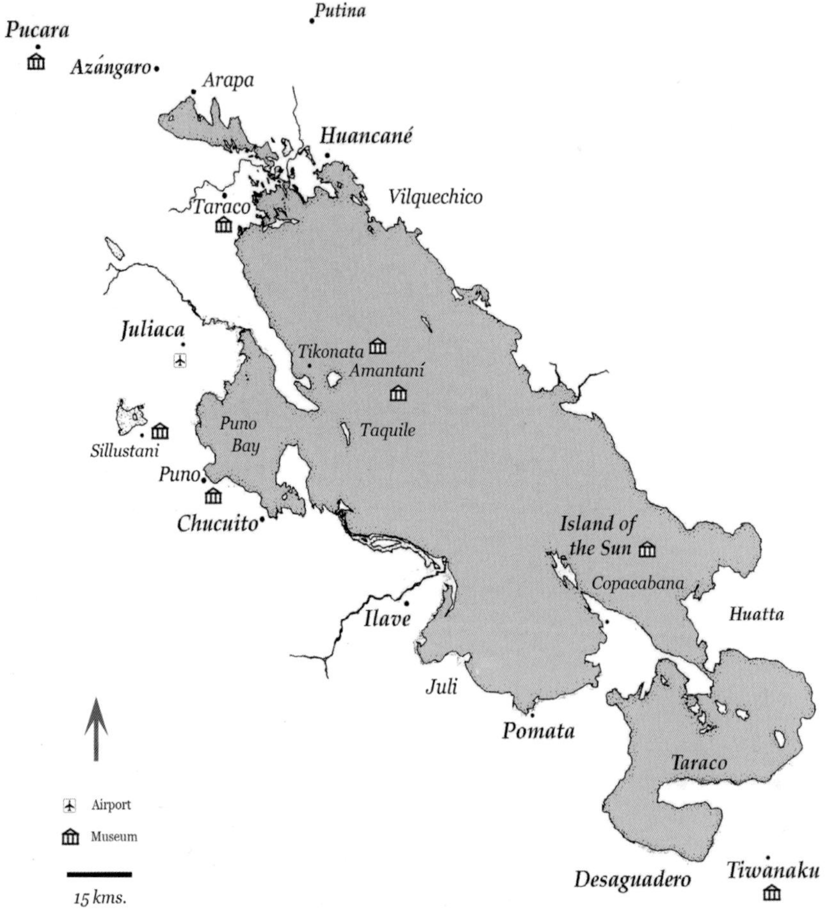

Pucara

Putina

Azángaro

Arapa

Huancané

Taraco

Vilquechico

Juliaca

✈ Airport

Tikonata

Amantaní

Sillustani

Puno
Bay

Taquile

Puno

Chucito

Island of
the Sun

Copacabana

Ilave

Huatta

Juli

Pomata

Taraco

Desaguadero

Tiwanaku

✈ Airport

🏛 Museum

15 kms.

Preface

This book distills our knowledge of the Titicaca region based upon the work of numerous scholars and colleagues over many decades. It is designed for the curious nonspecialist who has an interest in this fascinating area of the world. I am always struck by the reactions of first time visitors to the lake. People come with many expectations. Some come for adventure, some for spiritual fulfillment, some like me because we just love the area. Others are just passing through onto Cuzco or La Paz. In all my experience over the last 25 years, I rarely meet the traveler who is not amazed at the beauty and richness of the culture and history of Lake Titicaca. This book focuses on the peoples and ancient cultures of this fascinating area. I have lavishly illustrated the book as a way of bringing in the casual reader, but I have also provided sound academic information for those seeking a richer understanding of what they see when they visit this marvelous land.

The content of this book is based on many seasons of my own research in Moquegua, Puno, northern Chile and Bolivia. There are many people and institutions that have provided invaluable help. I wish to thank the Programa Contisuyu, and in particular, Michael Moseley, Don Rice, the late Victor Barua, Lucy Barua and Luis Watanabe for their help and friendship on my research from 1983 to 1985 in Moquegua. This experience was a phenomenal time in my life and set the stage for the creation of a similar research program in Puno.

In 1988, my colleagues and I began research near the town of Juli on the Peruvian side of Lake Titicaca, at the suggestion of the late John Hyslop. This work was funded by the Wenner-Gren Foundation for Anthropological Research, Patricia Dodson, and the Montgomery Fund of the Field Museum of Natural History in Chicago. By 1990, the Juli Project had evolved into the Lupaqa Project, a larger survey and excavation program in the Lupaqa area of the southwestern Titicaca Basin. In 1993-1994, we excavated two sites near the town of Juli and extended our survey work.

For my work in the Juli area, I offer a special thanks to officials of the National Institute of Culture and fellow archaeologists in Lima and Puno including Elias Mujica, Oscar Castillo, Oscar Ayca, and Luis Lumbreras. The Lupaqa Project was assisted by the anthropological faculty of the Universidad Nacional del Altiplano including its director, Felix Palacios, Juan Bautista Carpio Torres, and Abel Torres

Cornejo. Percy Che-Piu Salazar, Julio César Gómez Gamona, and Luis Salas Aronés supported our project as well. I also gratefully acknowledge the support of Fernando Cabieses and Walter G. Tapia Bueno. For their kindness and hospitality during this period, I thank Percy Calizaya Ch. and family, Fresia Gandarillas S., Moises Sardon P., and the people of Juli, Yacari-Tuntachawi, Sillucani, Inca Pucara, Huaquina, Chatuma, Pomata, and Checca Checca.

In 1994, Brian Bauer, Oswaldo Rivera, and I began the Proyecto Tiksi Kjarka on the Island of the Sun, Bolivia. Johan Reinhard graciously assisted our project on the islands, and I thank him for his collegiality. I also acknowledge the help of the Instituto Nacional de Arqueología and the Secretaría Nacional de Cultura, including Javier Escalante, Carlos Ostermann, and Oswaldo Rivera S. I returned to survey on the Peruvian side after our work on the Island of the Sun was finished in 1997. Together with Edmundo de la Vega and Cecília Chávez we created a new research entity named "Programa Collasuyu", a group of scholars that continue to work in the Titicaca region. In 1997, de la Vega and Chávez excavated on Estéves Island outside of Puno. Luis Vásquez and Mary Vásquez are gratefully acknowledged for their contributions to our work over the years. I likewise offer a personal thanks to Ken and Ligia Keller and their family for their gracious help and support over the years.

There are dozens of people whom I wish to acknowledge for their professional assistance, advice, friendship and collaboration over the last three decades. I thank Elizabeth Arkush, Kirk Frye, Elizabeth Klarich, Christopher Donnan, Mario Núñez, Aimée Plourde, Maria Cecilia Lozada, Lee Steadman, Luperio Onofre Mamani, Mark Aldenderfer, Brian Bauer, Mario Rivera, John Janusek, Clark Erickson, Ben Bronson, Eric Gardner, Shauna Mecartea, Evgenia Grigorova, Cheri Quinto, Amber Cordts-Cole, Laura Lliguin, Helle Girey, Jill Silton, Ran Boytner, Clark Erickson, Alexei Vranich, Chap Kusimba, Michael Moseley, Johan Reinhard, Tom and Alina Levy, Bob Adams, Charles Kolb, Chela Fattorini, Don Rice, Katharina Schreiber, Karen Wise, Christine Hastorf, Helaine Silverman, Paul Goldstein, Karl La Favre, Amanda Cohen, Carol Schultze, Abigail Levine, Robert Feldman, Garine Babian, Rita Lewis, Mark Kielar, Alessandro Duranti, and colleagues at both the Field Museum of Natural History and at UCLA. My dear friends Gregory Areshian and Larry Coben deserve thanks for their support over the years. I thank the late Craig

Morris of the American Museum of Natural History in New York for allowing me access to the Bandelier collection. I acknowledge the gracious professional help offered to our Esteves Island project by Mario Núñez of Puno. I would also like to offer my gratitude to Rolando Paredes, a great friend and great archaeologist. I also thank Lupe Andrade and her family and Ken and Ligia Keller and family for their support during my work in Bolivia. During the last dozen years, our work has shifted to the northern Titicaca Basin. This work, co-directed by Cecilia Chávez and me, benefitted from the professional work of Mike Henderson, Adan Umire, Javier Chalcha, and countless others over the years. I especially thank Joyce Marcus for her critical commentary, her friendship, and advice. She was a great friend during a semester I spent in Ann Arbor in 1983 as a graduate student, and she has continued to be a source of unwavering encouragement and support. Her advice has greatly improved the clarity and quality of my work.

Much of the work in Program Collasuyu could not have been accomplished without the support of Mr. and Mrs. Lloyd Cotsen. I again express my deep thanks and gratitude for their support of archaeology at UCLA. Mr. Cotsen has consistently encouraged archaeologists to be relevant to peoples' lives. This book is written in this spirit.

Finally, a heartfelt thanks to Cecilia Chávez, co-director of Programa Collasuyu, my colleague and close friends of many years.

My research over the years has been largely funded by the National Science Foundation and the Cotsen Endowments at UCLA. Additional funding was provided by the Wenner-Gren Foundation, Doherty Foundation, the Mellon Foundation of the University of Chicago, The H. John Heinz III Trust, the Field Museum of Natural History and several private donors including Ms. Patricia Dodson, Robert Donnelly, Deborah Arnold, Walt Zipperman, Charles Steinmetz, Harris Bass, Patty and Roger Civalleri, and David and Kathleen Boocheever.

All images are by the author unless noted. I acknowledge clker.com, Google, and Google Earth for use of public domain images. Errors in fact and interpretation are purely my responsibility.

Nestled in the high Andes at over 3,800 meters above the sea, the great Lake Titicaca is one of the most famous and mysterious bodies of water in the world. Lake Titicaca stretches over an area larger than 40 countries. It is one of the largest lakes in the world and is popularly known as the highest navigable lake on the planet. In the ancient Andes, the Titicaca region was an economic powerhouse supporting the development of dozens of civilizations. It was the birthplace of the sun and the moon for the Inca peoples of the fifteenth and sixteenth centuries. Like the Incas, the earlier Tiwanaku peoples worshipped a Sacred Rock on the Island of the Sun, which formed the center of their religious and political world. From the beginning of recorded history to the present day, fantastic stories about the Titicaca area abound.

The lake is over 200 kilometers in length and about 60 kilometers at its widest making it the second largest lake in South America surpassed in size only by Lake Maracaibo. Lake Titicaca is very deep, and its waters are very cold. In some areas in the middle of the lake, depths of over 250 meters have been recorded. The water fluctuates between 12 and 14 degrees centigrade—so cold that a strong swimmer could survive in the water only a short time. Exploration of the lake is therefore difficult, particularly given the high altitude and thin air. Because of these harsh conditions, there has been little underwater exploration. In fact, much of the lake bottom remains unexplored. In the deeper and least accessible parts of the lake, there almost certainly exist unrecorded fish and aquatic plant species. We actually know more about the surface of the moon than we know about the bottom of this vast highland lake.

The lake sits between two mountain chains. To the east is the imposing Cordillera Real, or Royal Mountains. Snowcapped mountain peaks rise to more than 5,500 meters before they quickly descend into the Amazonian drainage. To the west is the Cordillera Blanca, or White Mountains. These are the highest peaks one crosses before dropping down into the Pacific watershed. The entire Titicaca Basin—it is, in fact, a large geological "bowl" that was carved in the late Pleistocene epoch

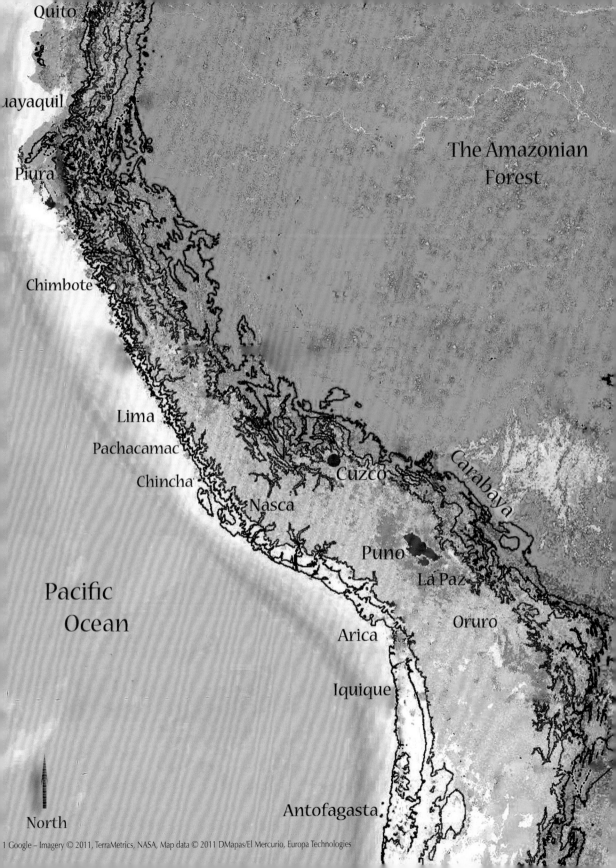

The beautiful Lake Titicaca with the Bolivian Cordillera Real in the background.

well before humans ever walked on the continent—covers a vast area of more than 50,000 square kilometers.

Long before Europeans arrived in the sixteenth century, the Titicaca region was a land of great power—political, economic, social, and spiritual. The Inca believed that the founding couple of their empire—Mama Ojila and Manco Capac—emerged from the Island of the Sun and then traveled north to Cusco to found their future empire. Throughout their short reigns, Inca emperors were obligated to make a long pilgrimage to the Island of the Sun and the Island of the Moon, to the ruined but ritually powerful city of Tiwanaku, and to the eastern side of the lake before their return trip to Cusco. Inca emperors married women from Tiwanaku, sought to have some of their sons and daughters conceived and born in the lake area, offered

The northern edge of the lake in a small bay near Vilquechico.

precious objects to the cold waters, and built a vast religious and political complex throughout the region. The most populous and productive province of the Inca Empire, known as Collasuyu, was also one of the most spiritual areas of the huge state, housing one of the three most important pilgrimage destinations, along with the oracle of Pachacamac on the Peruvian coast and the sacred caves of Paucaritambo near Cusco.

For anyone who visits this beguiling place, the Titicaca region becomes a source of mystery, intrigue, and fascination. Numerous legends and myths have sprung up about the peoples and the land of ancient Collasuyu. Divided in the sixteenth century between different political and ethnic groups, such as the Lupaqa in the west, the Colla to the north, and the Pacajes to the south, the region was rich in resources and cultural diversity. The lake area has also been central in some of the most enduring myths and legends of our time. In this book, we will begin with the peoples, cultures, and landscape of this fabulous world. We will then explore the modern myths and legends that have developed about the lake and the people

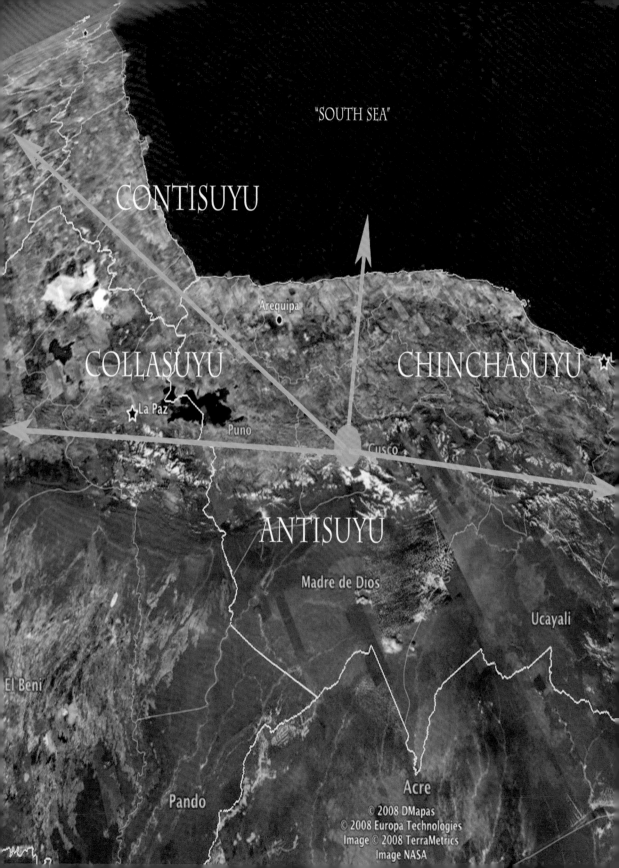

"SOUTH SEA"

CONTISUYU

Arequipa

COLLASUYU

CHINCHASUYU

La Paz

Puno

Cusco

ANTISUYU

Madre de Dios

Ucayali

El Beni

Pando

Acre

© 2008 DMapas
© 2008 Europa Technologies
Image © 2008 TerraMetrics
Image NASA

who inhabit it. We will take a brief trip through space and time, learning about the legends of lost Atlantis, Paititi, El Dorado, spaceships, underwater temples, and mysterious tunnels. We'll learn about the mythic theories of peripatetic Egyptians, Chinese, people from the mythical land of Lemuria, Polynesians, Easter Islanders, children of Israel, and even Jesus Christ.

We will finally arrive at the world of scholarly inquiry. In the end, I hope to leave the reader with a sense that the most fascinating story of all is that of science and the truly wondrous mysteries that it uncovers. We will see how the first peoples entered this harsh land more than 10 millennia ago. We will trace the rise of civilizations of unprecedented sophistication and beauty. We will learn how they moved multi-ton blocks with labor and ingenuity to build cities in the sprawling grasslands. We will see how the myths and legends, however beguiling, are just the beginning of a journey of discovery. The most spectacular story of all is not one of spacemen, but one discovered by scientific inquiry of the indigenous peoples of the Titicaca region who created this beguiling cultural, spiritual, and economic landscape without help from anyone outside their own rich world.

The Collao

The greater Titicaca region stretches over a vast area, from mountain chain to mountain chain from east to west and from the grasslands near La Raya in the north to the desert lands south of La Paz, Bolivia. The earliest references in the historic texts to this region call it the Collao, or land of the Colla peoples.[1] The name Collasuyu, in fact, translates into "quarter of the Colla" and was the Inca name for the rich southern part of their empire. The Inca conceptually divided their world -- Tawantinsuyu-- into four great quarters with Cusco as the center of the political body. In fact, Cusco was referred to as the "navel" of the universe emphasizing the human body metaphor common in ancient empires. Traditionally, the term Colla refers to both the people and the geographical region of the protohistoric and historic "kingdom" (*señorío*) that was located on the north side of Lake Titicaca.

Opposite: The Inca Empire or Tawantinsuyu as perceived from Cusco.

Two young merchants from the Island of the Sun in Bolivia pose next to an apacheta on the highest point on the island. Apachetas are cairns that function as roadside shrines and markers.

There is, in fact, some dispute about what exactly comprised the Collao in antiquity. Unlike modern Western states, the Incas and their ancestors generally did not have clearly defined borders and boundaries. They conceived of their provinces in ethnic and geographical terms and not strictly as physical places. The early Spanish historian Pedro Cieza de León tells us that the northern boundary of the Titicaca region was at the town of Ayaviri.[2] Other writers place the northern boundary at the famous pass at La Raya, located a few days' walk north of smaller Lake Arapa, the northernmost part of the chain of lakes that comprise Titicaca.[3] In fact, this pass is a major cultural and geographical boundary between the Cusco and Titicaca regions. It is over this pass that the Inca armies entered the Titicaca region in the mid- to late fifteenth century, rolling down through the present-day Santa Rosa area

Opposite: A yatiri, or religious specialist, on the Island of the Sun conducts a payment to the earth.

on toward Ayaviri. Cieza de León says that the boundary in the south is the town of Caracollo. This makes sense, and one can make the case that the "conceptual" southern boundary of the Titicaca region is found near Caracollo at the base of the great mountain Illimani, which towers over the modern city of La Paz.

For most of the year, the landscape of the Collao is dry. Vegetation is restricted to pockets where springs provide for small oases of life or where rivers and irrigation canals provide freshwater from the mountains. Serious rains begin in October. During the rainy season, the landscape blooms, transforming the desert into a wonderland of cultivated plants and wild pasture. In some years, such as in 2003, the lake rises several meters above normal, flooding large tracts of land. In normal years, people build nearer and nearer the lake edge. During the rare flood years, villages and evens towns can be flooded out.

These geographical and climatic conditions provide for a surprisingly diverse ecological mosaic around the Titicaca region. For instance, there are numerous bays and inlets along the lake edge. One of the largest bays is Puno, found on the

northwestern side. The protected waters provide an excellent location for the growth of reeds, fish, and other aquatic resources. Along with the bays are the rivers of freshwater that flow into the lake. These rivers were some of the first areas to be settled by ancient peoples. Rivers such as the Ramis in the north, the Escoma and Ilave in the center, and the Desaguadero and Katari in the south were in many ways the resources that made civilization possible.

There are as many theories about the ancient name of Titicaca as there are tour guides and scholars. The simple fact is that the ancient name of Lake Titicaca is not known. Given the fact that there were numerous and competing polities in the region during the protohistoric period (i.e., the century or so before European conquest), it is possible that there was no single, commonly accepted name even at the time of the Spanish conquest. Just as Iranians refer to the large body of water adjacent to them as the Persian Gulf, while the Saudis refer to the same body of water as the Arab Gulf, it appears there was no common, shared name for Lake Titicaca in the absence of a single cultural or political body that covered the lakeshore.[4]

What we do know is that the word titi is an Aymara term meaning "puma" or "mountain cat." This is confirmed in a dictionary published in 1612 by the great linguist Ludovico Bertonio. Bertonio lived and worked in the Titicaca region and compiled an exhaustive dictionary of Aymara that remains a primary source of information on the historic peoples of the region. The word titi is also listed as "lead" (plomo) by Bertonio or as "puma," "lead," or "a heavy metal" in some modern dictionaries.[5] Bertonio lists the word caca or kaka as "white or gray hairs of the head". Furthermore, the term k'ak'a, as used in the Omasuyus province to the east of the lake, is defined in a modern Aymara dictionary compiled by de Lucca as a "crack or fissure" or, alternatively, a "comb of a bird." Two informants of twentieth-century anthropologist Weston La Barre's said that the proper name of the lake was Titiq'aq'a, meaning "gray discolored, lead-colored puma," based upon a stone on the Island of the Sun in the south of the lake.[6]

Not all early named references to the lake include the term titi or caca. According to Diego de Alcobasa, the ancient name of Lake Titicaca was Chuquivitu.[7]

Previous: The famous mountain at the La Raya Pass between the Cusco and Puno regions.
Opposite Top: The pass below La Raya, with the town of Santa Rosa in the center.
Opposite Bottom: The great plains that stretch between La Raya and Ayaviri.

21

The high puna landscape above the lake.

Chuqui is defined by Bertonio as "lance"; vittu is listed as "the top of a hill."[8] In modern usage, the large lake is occasionally referred to as Lake Chucuito, and the small lake to the south is called Huiñamarca. Finally, the large lake is occasionally referred to as Lago Mayor and the small lake as Lago Menor. In other words, there probably was no commonly accepted name for the lake by all of the peoples that lived around it.

Some references in Bertonio's dictionary provide two hypotheses for the ancient name used most commonly in the region. Under the entry "Thakhsi cala," Bertonio lists the definition "*piedra fundamental*," evoking theological themes.[9] The word *cala* is consistently listed as "rock." Thakhsi is defined as "horizon" or "end of the earth" and as *cimiento*, meaning "foundation" or "fundamental principle." It is possible that the name Titicaca is a corruption of the term *thakhsi cala*, the fifteenth/

Opposite Top: A rich harvest of crops during the winter months.
Opposite Bottom: A rich harvest of quinoa on the fertile lake edge.

The northern Titicaca region near Huancané during the floods of 2003.

sixteenth-century name of the Sacred Rock and the island on which it is found. The Island of the Sun was, and occasionally still is, also known as Isla Titicaca. Early Spanish writers often used the name of the island for the lake as well. And the name of the Sacred Rock area was also used for the island as a whole. Therefore, the term *thakhsi cala* was corrupted into titicala and titicaca. Given that there was no common name for the lake, it is likely that the Spaniards used the name of the site of the most

Puno Bay and the town of Puno, located in the northwestern Titicaca region. Puno was an important area of metallurgy in the prehistoric and Colonial periods and a major way station in the Inca Empire.

important indigenous shrine in the region, the Island of the Sun, as the name for the lake as well.

A second hypothesis, favored by linguists, is the most commonly accepted one: that the word titi is the indigenous word for "sun." This could have been an Aymara word, or perhaps even Pukina or early Quechua. Pukina was a widespread language in the sixteenth century that mysteriously disappeared within three generations of Spanish rule. *Cala*, of course, is "rock," giving us the more common name Rock of the Sun. Using the same logic, the name of the most sacred place in the lake was transposed to the name of the lake itself. Certainly, after a few years of Spanish rule, the lake was consistently known as Titicaca, with the smaller lake in the south continuing to be called Huiñamarca.

Indigenous Peoples of the Titicaca Region

Pedro Cieza de León wrote in the 16th century that the Inca province of the Collao, formally called Collasuyu, was one of the richest and most densely populated provinces in all of Peru.[10] As we have seen, the heartland of the Collao is the Lake Titicaca basin, with the huge and beautiful lake in the center of the region itself. The vast grasslands, mountains, and deserts that surround the lake comprise the rest of Collasuyu. During the sixteenth century, early Spanish historians referred to a number of peoples and languages in the region, the most notable being the Aymara,

A reed boat on one of the Uru islands in Puno Bay. Photo courtesy María Cecilia Lozada.

Pukina, Quechua, and Uru. The Aymara are the descendants of the protohistoric fifteenth-century peoples who built the largest and most powerful Titicaca regional polities. Most scholars argue that the earlier cultures of the region, such as Tiwanaku, were also Aymara speakers, although there is some disagreement on this point.[11] There is no question, however, that Aymara speakers of the Titicaca region dominated the political landscape of the region for at least 400 years prior to the Inca conquest in the fifteenth century and were the principal ethnic and language group in the pre-Hispanic south-central Andes. Once the Inca crossed beyond the Canas and Canchis territories to the northwest of La Raya in the late fifteenth or very early sixteenth century, they conquered and brought with them many Quechua-speaking colonists. Today the northern part of the lake has a large number of Quechua

The bustling town of Juliaca is a major commercial center in the Peruvian highlands.

speakers. Pockets of Quechua speakers are also found throughout the area well to the south of the Titicaca region, most notably in the Cochabamba area of Bolivia. The Quechua speakers found in the southern Titicaca region are most likely remnants of transplanted colonists from the Inca Empire who adopted the Titicaca region as their home.

Another group of people, the Uru, are much more enigmatic. In fact, many scholars believe they are not even an ethnic group like the Aymara and Quechua. The origin and history of these perennially marginalized and oppressed people remain some of the most vexing problems in Titicaca Basin linguistics and anthropology. Smaller ethnic groups and/or languages in the region include the Pukina, Uruquilla, Chipaya, and Choquela. Pukina is now an extinct language. In the sixteenth century,

Opposite: Young people in Taraco on market day. Many people in the region have two homes—one in a small village and another in a town.
Following page: A caravan in the high puna near Mazo Cruz.

however, it was widespread throughout large areas of the south-central Andes.[12] Uruquilla was also much more widespread in the past. Finally, sixteenth-century documents make reference to people who came from around the entire south central Andes from as far away as the Amazonian Basin. The Titicaca region was truly a complex, multi-cultural landscape throughout it history.

One fascinating feature of the Titicaca region is that people are characteristically multi- or bilingual. The rise of nationalism in Europe in the nineteenth century colors our view of what ancient societies were like. Europeans came to correlate a single language with a single ethnicity and political unit. It was in this context that the concept of the "nation" was born. In reality, most of the pre-modern world, in the West and the rest of the world, was multilingual and the western concept of a nation was quite foreign.

In the Titicaca region, it is still very common to meet people who speak Quechua, Aymara, and Spanish. In sixteenth- and early-seventeenth-century documents, particularly church surveys conducted to know what languages were necessary for the priests to know in each town, it was rare to find a place where only one language was spoken. In most cases, a village had at least two or three different languages spoken, including Aymara, Pukina, Quechua, and Uruquilla. Bi- and tri-lingualism are common characteristics of the peoples of the Titicaca region and this multilingual tradition has deep historical roots. When we try to understand the complex ethnic mix in the region, it is important to realize that people were multilingual and lived in multiple villages and towns.

Aymara peoples call their language *haque aru* meaning "language of the people" or "language of the Indians," or simply "human language."[13] The greatest concentration of modern Aymara speakers in the Titicaca region is along the lakeshore, particularly on the western and southern sides. Modern Aymara speakers are concentrated in two Titicaca region cities, Puno and Juliaca, and in a number of towns, villages, and hamlets throughout Peruvian and Bolivian territory. In Puno and Juliaca, the Aymara share neighborhoods with Quechua speakers, and virtually everyone now speaks Spanish as a first or second language. Most of the larger towns on the Peruvian side are also listed in sixteenth-century documents as former Lupaqa or Colla settlements, central towns for the Aymara *señoríos*, or kingdoms, of the time. These towns include Hatuncolla, Chucuito, Acora, Ilave, Juli, Pomata, Zepita, Yunguyu, and Desaguadero. On the Bolivian side there are a number of towns of substantial size, including Escoma, Kasani, Ancoraimes, Guaqui, and Copacabana.

Opposite: The Tarapacá Valley in northern Chile is typical of the coastal valleys
where Pukina and probably other now-extinct languages were spoken.

3 2

The origin of Aymara speakers in the Titicaca region is a subject of considerable debate. Generally, linguists and some anthropologists argue that Aymara speakers arrived relatively late in prehistory, during the immediate pre-Inca period around the thirteenth or fourteenth century, as aggressors into territory settled by Pukina speakers.[14] Most archaeologists, however, believe that the Tiwanaku, Pucara, and Taraceño peoples in the first millennium AD spoke an ancient variety of Aymara along with several other languages, as mentioned above. My own view is that the archaeological perspective, combined with linguistic information, is correct: the ancestors of the Aymara built the great kingdom of Tiwanaku and were there for centuries prior to European contact.

Throughout the greater Titicaca region, there are dozens of places where Quechua is the dominant language. As mentioned above, the distribution of Quechua in the east, west, and south Titicaca region is viewed by most archaeologists as the product of Inca colonization policies in the fifteenth century. The administrators of the Inca Empire placed colonists throughout the region for military, strategic, and

economic purposes. In the early Colonial documents for the Titicaca region, for instance, we occasionally find references to immigrant "Chinchasuyus" in places like the town of Juli. This would refer to the generic name of peoples from Chinchasuyu, the large northwestern quarter of the Inca Empire. Such information tells us that the empire brought people from as far as perhaps the Chimu kingdom, centered in modern Trujillo, to the Titicaca basin. This is a distance of at least 1300 kilometers, a truly remarkable effort to resettle peoples.

Linguists generally have some very different views than archaeologists, arguing that Aymara is much later in prehistory and that forms of ancestral Quechua existed prior to the Inca conquest of the region. These and many other kinds of scholarly problems are still being investigated in the area. We can say that in the far northern Titicaca Basin, near Ayaviri, there is little disagreement about the presence of Quechua speakers. The modern distribution of Quechua most certainly represents the ancestral distribution of Quechua from at least the thirteenth century, if not earlier. However, as we go farther south, the scholarly disagreements about the language of Tiwanaku, the protohistoric peoples prior to the Inca, and even the Inca themselves are increasingly heated and interesting.

The Uru are one of the more enigmatic groups in the region. The modern Uru are a famous tourist attraction, living on artificial islands in Lake Titicaca, subsisting as fishers and on tourist income. They speak Aymara and Spanish and most have houses in Puno. Apart from small groups of Aymara-speaking Uru living on the island outside Puno, there are no existing Uru enclaves in the Titicaca region. The anthropologist Weston La Barre listed a number of Uru enclaves in the nineteenth century, but these groups appear to have been acculturated into the dominant Aymara society by the time he did his research in the 1930s.[15]

The Uru are traditionally described as impoverished and marginal members of Titicaca society, usually associated with fishing and houses in the water. The Garci Diez de San Miguel Visita of 1567 refers to the Uru as poor and landless. The Visita is a comprehensive document compiled by a Spanish bureaucrat for tax purposes. It provides census data and the results of interviews conducted by this royal official in the 1560s. One notable indigenous leader, Martín Cari of Chucuito, an Aymara-speaking chief or cacique, referred to Urus as fishermen and poor. He said, "[T]here are five other ayllu [native social groups] of fishermen indians that are called by another name uros that are poor people who do not have farms but subsist only by fishing and by go about in the lake."[16] The association of fishing with poverty and low status is curious, given that coastal Andean populations held fishers in higher regard and exported dried fish into the sierra.[17] This difference is most likely a result of the different cultural attitudes of people living in the vast desert coasts of Peru and Chile at this time from those living in the highlands such as the Titicaca Basin.

Linguistically and conceptually, the Uru were consistently associated with the lake, more specifically with water. For instance, one term in Bertonio's dictionary is *uma haque*, defined as "anyone that deals with the sea, or lake, such as mariners, uru, etc." The word *uma* is the Aymara term for "water," and the word *haque* means "people." In a similar manner, one definition of uru is "a nation of poor indians that ordinarily are fishermen."[18] The one constant in the early documents is the association between the Uru and water.

At first analysis, it would appear that the Uru were merely an impoverished ethnic group speaking their own language and existing on the margins of the dominant Aymara society. One of the most fascinating ideas concerning the Uru was initially suggested by José Camacho and John Murra and elaborated by a number of later scholars.[19] These scholars argue that the designation "Uru" is a social status and tax category, not an ethnic one. In this view, the Uru were simply Aymara speakers placed in a different socioeconomic and, by extension, tax category. In the words of Bruce Mannheim, a linguist, "Uru designated an organizational and functional position in the economy, rather than a language."[20]

A fascinating and famous piece of evidence for this view is a case where a group of apparently wealthy Uru petitioned the Spanish state to be reclassified as Aymara. Reclassified Uru had to actually pay more taxes. Why would anybody seek to pay more tribute unless such a "privilege" conferred certain advantages? The answer is contained in a very important reference in the Garci Diez Visita. The

A magnificent terraced hill near Lake Arapa in the northern Titicaca Basin. An early temple was located on the hilltop more than 2,000 years ago.

Corregidor or chief administrator of the Chucuito province, Ruiz de Estrada, said that "each town serves its tambo [Inca storage building] and that this service is usually done by the Uros indians because they are poor."

As a mistreated, poor minority, the Uru were relegated to the menial tasks within the taxation system. A reclassification to Aymara status permitted people to meet their tribute obligations by providing goods, such as wool and camelids, without having to provide labor. In some instances, we see that Aymara quickly adapted and paid their taxes in actually Spanish money. Freed from labor obligations, individual Aymara households could amass additional wealth from their herds and fields. In other words, while an Aymara designation required a higher tax rate, it also conferred certain privileges that included freedom from labor taxes and the

Opposite: Two women from the northern Basin.
Following page: A herd of llamas and alpacas.

Totora reeds are among the most important natural products of the region.

ability to use labor to produce more personal wealth. It was a tax worth paying and a higher status worth claiming. Over time, there would have been a distinct advantage to paying taxes in-kind as opposed to paying in labor. This would account for the seemingly illogical request on the part of some Uru to be reclassified as Aymara. "Uru" was a social designation of poverty, reflecting a social prejudice that has been barely erased even in the twenty-first century.

Another mysterious language is Pukina. The language is now almost extinct, and little is known about its grammar and vocabulary.[21] Sixteenth-century documents indicate that this language was widely spoken in the southern part of the central Andes. It was one of three "general" languages of Peru, along with Quechua and Aymara. Most linguists argue that Quechua and Aymara belong to separate language

Opposite: A small community near Chucuito where a cemetery shares space with drying reeds.

families.[22] There is substantial literature on these two languages, and their syntaxes and lexicons are relatively well understood. The situation with Pukina is different. There is no comprehensive lexicon, and very little of its grammar and vocabulary are known. The early writer Geronimo de Ore published a book in Naples called Rituale seu Manuale Peruanum in 1607. This book contained about 30 pages in Pukina, including the Lord's Prayer, with translations into other languages. The Ore manuscript essentially provides the only Pukina vocabulary compiled from original speakers.[23] Scholars generally recognize that suffixes such as baya and paya are Pukina place-names, leftovers from prehispanic periods. These names are found throughout the region, most famously in a large arc that starts on the Bolivian side of the lake near the village of Batallas and goes over the northwestern top of Lake Titicaca and then back south into Carumas, Arequipa, and Moquegua. Place-names such as Chiribaya, Porobaya, Ilibaya, Paralaque, and so forth are found throughout this area.

One of the great tragic consequences of the spread of our modern global culture is the disappearance of so many smaller languages. The Titicaca region was

home to many small languages, most of which have disappeared. The sixteenth-century documents talk about an ethnic group called the Huruquilla, located in small pockets along the southern and southwestern Lake Titicaca shore. Some anthropologists think the Uruquilla are actually the modern Chipaya. The Chipaya are one of the lesser-known ethnic groups in the Titicaca region. The location of early historic Uruquilla speakers and the apparent linguistic similarity between Uruquilla and Pukina (in contrast to the different language family of Aru/Jaqi, to which Aymara belongs)[24] suggest to some linguists a relatively recent (post–AD 1000) contact between Aymara and non-Aymara speakers in the greater Titicaca area.[25] Based on these historical linguistic patterns, we can hypothesize that the twelfth- to fifteenth-century distribution of Uruquilla speakers would have been more extensive and would have covered the area southeast of the Rio Desaguadero into what is today extreme southeastern Peru, northwestern Bolivia, and northern Chile.

Virtually all societies have people who seek to get away from cities and the control of authorities. The Titicaca region is no different. Early documents from the area occasionally talk about groups of hunters who lived in the high puna, far away from settled towns and the oppressive yoke of the church and state. In Bertonio's dictionary, a people called the Choquela were defined as "wild or renegade people [called *cimarron* in Spanish] who live in the puna sustaining themselves by hunting." Other terms in Bertonio's dictionary designate people living outside established villages and political structures. The terms *huacora* and *kita* are defined as a "wild person" or "fugitive." An Aymara ritual hunting dance, described by Harry Tschopik and Cuentas Ormachea, is also called Choquela. The ceremony was practiced in the towns of Juli, Ichu, Chucuito and western Bolivia in the early to mid-twentieth century, according to Tschopik and Bandelier. José Huidobro, Freddy Arce, and Pasqual Quispe describe a Choquela dance on the Island of the Sun, where it commemorates the ritual hunting of vicuña after the agricultural harvest. Tschopik notes that it takes place on hilltops and includes ritual hunting songs and pantomimes of the hunt. At the end of the ceremony, the vicuña is killed. It is fascinating that

Opposite: A typical reed boat, traditionally used for fishing and local transport.

43

The bustling market in Taraco.

a sixteenth-century word describing "wild" hunters is the same as the name of a ritual hunting ceremony of the twentieth century. While this twentieth-century ethnography certainly does not prove the existence of pre-sixteenth-century hunting peoples, it certainly suggests that the term Choquela is associated with such lifeways, as many scholars have suggested.[26]

The market in Puno with fruits brought in from farms in the eastern forests of Carabaya and Sandia.

Cuentas Ormachea provides the best description of the modern term Choquela.[27] He notes that the term has various meanings in the altiplano but is strongly connected with a propitiatory dance and the communal hunting of wild animals. He tells us that the dance is found only in Aymara-speaking communities of the altiplano, including towns as far north as Huancané and as far south as Pizacoma

near the international border. Likewise, on the Island of the Sun, local informants use the term Choquela to describe dances still conducted in the region. One can imagine that the arrival of the Spaniards and their onerous taxes and labor service in the mines, spurred many a young man to run away to the far-off regions of the mountains. The Aymara were very successful at negotiating their position in Inca and later Peruvian and Bolivian society. It is humorous that in the Garci Diez Visita, the Spanish administrator often comments on how odd it was that there were so many widows and children but so few men of taxable age in the towns and villages that he visited. Apparently always one step ahead of the assessor, the young men would disappear into the wilderness until Garci Diez de San Miguel left, successfully keeping themselves off of the tax roles.

In sum, during the Spanish conquest in the early to mid-sixteenth century, there were three major languages in the central Andes: Quechua, Aymara, and Pukina, along with a number of lesser ones, such as Uruquilla. The Uru represented marginalized peoples in the Titicaca area and were not primarily Pukina speakers. Rather, "Uru" was a social and taxation category and applied to poor people who spoke any number of indigenous languages. The Lake Titicaca region was a wonderful tapestry of ethnic groups and languages that formed over the millennia.

Society and Religion

The peoples of the Titicaca region have survived for thousands of years as farmers, herders, fishers, producers of goods, and traders. The climate of the region is central to their livelihood and their lives. The Titicaca area is relatively dry from April to September (though a brief period in August has rains), with serious rains beginning in October. During the rainy season, the landscape blooms with plants. Some of the mainstays of the highland Andean economy are llamas and alpacas, which have been replaced somewhat by European cattle and sheep. The rich lake edge also provides abundant resources, including reeds, fish, and countless kinds of foraging plants. Introduced lake trout is the principal fish grown and caught in the lake today.

Previous Photos:
Page 46-47: Dancers from the island of Tikonata.
Page 48. Dancers from Tikonata (top) and Arapa (bottom by A. Umire).
Page 49: A capilla in the Mazo Cruz area (upper) and a small shrine inside a capilla near Taraco (lower).
Page 50-51: Three young merchants on the Island of the Sun.

Archaeological excavations have uncovered countless quantities of indigenous fish species in the remains of the villages and hamlets that dotted the landscape before the introduction of trout. Trade, a mainstay of highland Andean economies for millennia, is as vigorous today as it was in the past. Either in the villages as in the days of old or in the modern central market in Puno, people move goods and wares from all over the region, from forest, mountains and desert, to trade with the many different peoples that they encountered throughout this vast land.

The Aymara and Quechua peoples of the region live a rich life, and they jealously guard their cultural values. Throughout the year, their private lives are filled with family and communal festivities, many now linked to the Christian calendar. Communal performances are particularly important. Tinku, a form of dance performed and enjoyed on an annual basis, has been part of the cultures for centuries. Tinku is traditionally a form of ritual battle, a tradition that began centuries or even millennia ago. Other holidays are celebrated with a variety of dances, music, food and drink. Unlike mainstream Western religious services, which are solemn and quiet (certain Baptist sects excepted), Aymara and Quechua religious ceremony is more typical of religions around the world. People laugh and enjoy one another's company while the religious specialists perform sacred rites. Only in a few cases is absolute quiet demanded. Cultural misunderstandings often occur between local peoples and visitors who do not understand the customs of the Titicaca region. Foreigners often see people enjoying themselves at what appears to be a festive occasion and do not realize that for local peoples, the occasion might be a very religious event.

Religion in the region is a mix of Christianity and indigenous beliefs. The landscape is dotted with small churches or capillas, a tradition that may be derived from the still-common practice of building *apachetas*, or cairns. These piles of rocks serve many purposes, including demarcating land, marking roads, and being areas where offerings are made. *Apachetas* are found everywhere on the hilltops, and most have the remains of offerings, usually bottles and some coca leaves. Shrines to celebrate the Christian God and the many saints are found throughout the cities, as well as in the villages, throughout the highlands and into the deserts. Pilgrimages

The beautiful Mount Illimani, the southernmost limit of the Titicaca cultural area.

to hilltop shrines are common. These pilgrimages coincide with Christian holidays and emphasize the hybrid nature of Aymara religious practices. One of the most important rituals is the indigenous *pago*, or payment to the earth. A ritual specialist will perform a rite that can take only a few minutes or several hours, depending upon the importance of the occasion.

Among the Aymara, the *yatiri*, or religious specialist, will conduct the ceremony. The word *yatiri* is not exactly translated as "shaman," as many people believe. The term actually refers to specialists in a number of tasks—something like the term doctor in Western culture, which can refer to physicians, dentists, chiropractors, and even college professors. *Yatiris* have prestige in their communities and have to successfully practice their art for years before they are accepted as truly expert. Each village or barrio often has many *yatiris*, and they often specialize in different ceremonies. It is particularly important to have a successful *pago* prior to digging into the earth or starting on a new construction or task of any significance, and a successful pago requires a knowledgeable yatiri to perform it.

A *pago* can be very simple and short, or it can be elaborate. As an archaeologist who has worked and excavated throughout the Titicaca region, I have hired many yatiris to conduct *pagos* prior to my work. It is not only a form of respect to the community but also an essential first step for any visitor to conduct such an activity. The *yatiri* will first interview the person requesting the ceremony. He or she will then provide a list of items to buy in local stores. These usually include llama fetuses, candies, wine, beer, colas, coca, small objects, and candles.[28] For divination pagos, the *yatiri* might request nuts or other objects to be read at the time of the rite. Every *yatiri* has his or her own set of items. There is also a hierarchy of *yatiris* in each community. The more respected the *yatiri*, the higher the price. For those who see this as a form of commercialization of religion, I remind them of the cost of hiring a priest, pastor, or rabbi for a wedding or other celebration in Western culture. It is effectively the same kind of phenomenon, with the same kind of effect. In a Western culture, including cities such as Lima or Arequipa, if a foreigner arrived and hired a local priest for a wedding or other ceremony, it would send the message that he or she respected the community by following its norms or customs. The same holds true for the more rural areas of the Titicaca basin.

The *yatiri* will determine the time and place of a large and complex pago, such as that for opening up an archaeological investigation. An individual may indeed be paying the *yatiri*, but the *yatiri* works for both the person and the community. In effect, the *yatiri* insures that the community's mores and wishes are followed. He or she has the authority to declare that a rite was a success or failure. In the latter case, the work cannot go on until more discussions are held. Imagine hiring a priest to officiate at a wedding, and, after due consideration, he declared that someone or something was not appropriate and stopped the ceremony. *Yatiris* have the same authority, and I have experienced several failed *pagos*, requiring more community consultation before I could go on with my work. It is an ingenious social institution that allows the community to express its dissatisfaction while at the same time insuring that no one person has to take the blame.

If all goes well, the *yatiri* will spend some time preparing the *pagos*. At this time, members of the community will congregate. The person paying for the *pagos* is expected to provide food and drink (as at a good wedding or funeral in other cultures). As mentioned before, a *pagos* is not a quiet, reflective moment; rather, people enjoy one another's company and check whether the ceremony is sufficiently opulent for the occasion. In fact, it is quite a jovial occasion, sometimes confusing tourists who expect everything to be solemn. Eventually, the *yatiri* will conduct the ceremony. In divination ceremonies, the articles purchased by the sponsor will be wrapped in paper and set on ichu grass or some other natural tinder. The culmination of the ceremony is a burning of the offering and a reading of the result. If the *yatiri* declares that all went well, work can proceed. If he declares that the ceremony was not acceptable, the sponsor has to perform another or several more pagos until the result is acceptable to the *yatiri* and the community that he or she represents.

Opposite: One of the massive chulpas or burial towers at the national archaeological park of Sillustani.

LEGENDS AND MYTHS

For the first-time visitor, the Titicaca region is indeed a place of great mystery and sublime beauty. From the vast plains of Ayaviri in the north to the southern deserts around Illimani, the altiplano holds surprises at almost every turn. The great forests over the mountains to the east were virtually uninhabited in the seventeenth and eighteenth centuries due to horrific plagues and economic changes brought by the Europeans—changes that killed and displaced many native peoples. Abandoned and sparsely populated places such as the eastern slope forests inevitably give rise to new legends and myths. It is no coincidence that many of the great gold mines of the Inca were found in the eastern slopes in Carabaya, Larecaja, and Sandia. Gold deposits inevitably attract the adventurous and the venal, and provide the stuff of myth and legend for generations.

The lake itself is large, deep, dark, and imposing. There are small villages, isolated hamlets, and people virtually hidden from view in this vast area of mountains, rivers, gorges, and desolate pampas. Evidence of ancient peoples is found all around the lake and in the hills above. Prehistoric roads are lined with ruins. Small towns have Inca and pre-Inca walls right in the streets that are littered with ancient pottery fragments. Vast areas of ancient raised fields are spread over the landscape attesting to the genius of the ancient peoples of the Titicaca basin.

Outsiders' ignorance of the Titicaca region and a lack of scientific research have spawned a virtual industry of modern myth making. It is truly amazing how many fairy tales have been created for this part of the world. We find in the travel and New Age literature statements such as this: "Many of the world's spiritual leaders, as well as indigenous teachers, acknowledge that the energy of the planet shifted in 1987 from the masculine energies of Tibet to the feminine energies of Peru, and more particularly, Lake Titicaca, Machu Picchu, and The Sacred Valley of the Incas."[29] Another Web writer claims, "Lake Titicaca is the preeminent holy place of all ancient Andean cultures and the source of a hundred cosmogenic myths."[30] We also learn about a great flood and that the pan-Andean creator god Viracocha emerged from the lake, going first to the Island of the Sun and later to Tiwanaku.

This is part of the "cataclysmic literature"—the idea that the world is beset with periodic catastrophic events that completely reshape history. While having no real scientific basis, this literature is very popular with people who seek commonalities in all the great religions and myths of the modern world to prove the existence of Atlantis, Mu, and other fantasies. The Titicaca region is central to many of these ideas, particularly the famous site and culture of Tiwanaku. The Web site just cited goes on to say that Tiwanaku "is on a planetary grid system aligned to the Yukon pole. This prehistoric grid system was operative two pole positions back in time, before the pole was at either its present location or its Hudson Bay position during the Antlantean epoch."[31] The precise planetary grid system is not revealed, of course, but the idea is that Tiwanaku was part of some set of linked cataclysms in the past, going back 96,000 years, in this case to the continent of Mu or Lemuria. From a scientific perspective, this notion is quite absurd, given that the first peoples to migrate to the Americas came no earlier than 20,000 or so years ago.

Lake Titicaca attracts many visitors seeking answers to timeless spiritual questions. According to this nonscientific literature, the Andes were formed with the destruction of the ancient mythical continent of Lemuria about 30,000 years ago.[32] The ancient city of Tiwanaku was one of Lemuria's most important colonies, which at the time were located on the shores of the Pacific Ocean. As the city of Tiwanaku rose up with the mountains, it became a refuge for those fleeing the floods and destruction. The great Lord Meru, Manu of the Sixth Ray, came to Tiwanaku and established the Monastery of the Brotherhood of the Seven Rays. This monastery, located in an undisclosed location in the lake region, holds the secrets of the lost continent of Mu, Atlantis, and other civilizations now forever gone. In particular, this perennially undiscovered monastery has a great solar disc, a cosmic Rosetta stone of sorts, that contains the answers to universal mysteries.

This spiritual travel literature commonly says that Tiwanaku was once at sea level and has since risen to its present altitude. This bizarre notion was actually

proposed by the Bolivian archaeologist Arthur Posnansky in the early part of the twentieth century. Posnansky had a number of strange ideas, among them that all civilizations of the Americas began in Tiwanaku when it was on the coast. Today, of course, we know that the uplift of the Andes started around 25,000,000 years ago, in the far geological past. The Andes looked like they do today millions of years before humans arrived on the continent. The idea that Tiwanaku was at one time a coastal city, or even a port on Lake Titicaca, is simply wrong and represents completely discredited speculations by an untrained amateur (albeit a flamboyant and influential one), almost one hundred years ago.

The fascination with lost continents and ambitiously peripatetic Old World peoples begins with some of the first histories written in the New World. The legend of the biblical land of Ophir, for instance, was a major theme of the early Spanish chroniclers, who were obsessed with religious themes. Ophir is mentioned only briefly in the Bible, yet it was a source of great speculation and rumor in the Americas. Specifically, Ophir was a faraway land mentioned in the Old Testament. King Solomon commissioned Phoenician ships to bring back gold to build the temple in Jerusalem, as described in this passage from 1 Kings 9:26–27: "King Solomon also built ships in Ezion Geber, which is located near Elat [Eilat] in the land of Edom, on the shore of the Red Sea. Hiram sent his fleet and some of his sailors, who were well acquainted with the sea, to serve with Solomon's men. They sailed to Ophir, took from there four hundred twenty units of gold, and then brought them to King Solomon." Based on this passage, some people have suggested that the Americas were in fact Ophir, the land of sun and gold. While dismissed by almost all educated people today, the idea was a source of major debate among Europeans in the Spanish colonial period.

On the surface, the debate would appear to be an arcane and minor theological point of the late sixteenth and early seventeenth century. But the debate had and still has significant political repercussions. Most important was the conclusion by some seventeenth-century scholars that Christ had come to the Americas. Those who asserted church and crown authority over indigenous peoples did not accept this argument, while those who sided with the local feudal aristocracy—the families of the conquistadores and early Spanish elite—largely accepted this fact. The Catholic Church provided much support for the theologians and historians who disagreed with the Ophir argument—since if the peoples of the Americas had rejected Christ, they could legally be enslaved by the local feudal aristocracy. If, however, they had not been given the opportunity to accept Christ, responsibility for their evangelization and control fell largely to the church, with the support of the crown. This seemingly esoteric point was hugely consequential to all the peoples of the New World. As strange as this appears to modern eyes, the question as to whether a whole continent of proud peoples would be enslaved by a theocracy or a feudal aristocracy depended to some degree on whether the principal Christian God had paid a visit to the Americas 1,500 years earlier.

By the nineteenth century, the vast majority of Western theologians agreed that Christ did not come to the Americas. However, at least one mainstream Western religion, the Church of Latter Day Saints (LDS), accepts the idea that Christ came to the New World. According to the Book of Mormon, a group of Jewish people left the Old World for Mesoamerica, arriving around 598 BC. They apparently settled in modern-day southern Mexico, Guatemala, and Belize. These people were called the Nephites. Other peoples included the Jaredites, who left Mesopotamia after the fall of Babel. These pre-Columbian peoples had writing, were white, and had direct and apparently continuous contact with the eastern Mediterranean. According to earlier LDS traditions, the Nephites and Jaredites arrived in an empty land and expanded over the whole of the Americas. In this reading, the ancient Titicaca people were also Nephites or Jaredites—at least up to around AD 385, when the Nephites were destroyed by the Lamanites. More recent LDS writers argue that there were probably other peoples in the Americas when the Nephites arrived, making the status of the Titicaca-area people a matter of some dispute in this theological tradition. At least one contemporary LDS writer claims that he discovered big skulls in burial towers in the great ancient cemetery at Sillustani near Puno in the 1970s. These burial towers are called chulpas today. The writer claims that the skulls were the remains

of Jaredites who inhabited Peru prior to European conquest, an idea that the LSD Church apparently still teaches.[33]

Jesus Christ is not the only foreigner who allegedly visited the Americas to bring civilization and enlightenment. Serious people have argued with great passion that Vikings, Africans, Chinese, Phoenicians, Greeks, Irish, Romans, Egyptians, Polynesians, East Indians, the armies of Alexander the Great, and others too numerous to remember visited the Americas. One of my favorite stories within this tradition is that of extraterrestrial (ET) visitors. Perhaps the best ET story of Lake Titicaca basin cultural origins is that of Akakor. According to this legend, a soon-to-be-murdered German journalist named Karl Brugger met an Indian man named Tatunca Nara, the chief of the lost Ugha Mongulala tribe, in a Brazilian bar named (I couldn't possibly make this up) Gracas a Deus.[34] According to the allegedly indigenous chief (who later was proven by a German publication to have had at least one German parent), white men in flying saucers arrived in the Amazon several thousand years ago to teach people how to live like civilized beings. They established three main cities, the principal one being Akakor, located somewhere near the Peru–Brazil border. Another of these cities was apparently Tiwanaku. At least 26 other cities, including the legendary town of Paititi and the actual ruined city of Machu Picchu, were built around Akakor. The spacemen also built a series of underground cities connected by tunnels throughout the Amazon and into Lake Titicaca.

In 2000 a group of amateur enthusiasts known as Akakor Geographical Exploring said in a press release that they had discovered an underwater temple in Lake Titicaca. After much excitement in the international press (the story was apparently picked up by a naive news stringer for a major network) and denunciations by the great Bolivian archaeologist Carlos Ponce Sanguines, the reality turned out to be substantially less exciting. Little has been heard about this discovery since, but it is likely that the "temple" was one of the abandoned piers or other modern constructions often found in the shallow areas of the lake.

The legend of Paititi, or El Dorado, is another story that has captured the imagination of foreigners for centuries. According to the legend, Paititi was a city built by renegade or fleeing Inca royalty and their followers on the eastern slopes of the Andes or in the forests. Many people connect the Akakor legend with those of the lost continent of Mu and Paititi. They claim there are tunnels under the mountains connecting the Atacama Desert with Lake Titicaca and Paititi. In fact, the idea that the area is full of hidden tunnels is one of the most enduring "urban legends" in the Titicaca region. Tunnels are said to run from the lake to Cusco, from the lake to Oruro, from churches, from city halls, and so on. Once I was accused of grinding pottery to extract gold (the shiny stuff in the pot sherds was actually montmorillonite mica, a decidedly nonprecious mineral) and shipping it via a submarine through a tunnel to the Pacific coast. Otherwise perfectly serious people will say with great conviction that they know of tunnels connecting the Island of the Sun with Cusco, or Puno with La Paz. The theme of underground passages is a constant one in Titicaca Basin culture. While one cannot prove a negative of this type, there are no recorded tunnels of any great length in the area. It is possible that the numerous mines and hidden chambers under churches are partially responsible for these stories. Many colonial-period houses have underground wine storage rooms that might have been connected by short tunnels. Once one of these tunnels is discovered, the rumors run rampant and further feed the myths that have been around for centuries.

The site of Chucuito, located about 16 kilometers from Puno, houses a very curious Inca temple filled with phallic-shaped stones. This temple, known in the scientific literature as Inca Uyu, is a vortex known as the Temple of Fertility in the New Age world.[38] As one tour Web site puts it, entering Chucuito, you are "now in the realm of Mama Cocha (Mother Lake), the feminine energy vortex of the Andes."[39] Inca Uyu is properly translated as "the Inca's corral or cemetery,"[40] but clever tour companies and other promoters have renamed it Inka Uyo (supposedly "the Inca's penis" in Quechua). The site is indeed spectacular and commands the attention of quite a few tourists.

The Lake Titicaca region is central in virtually all the fantastic legends told about the Andes. The Inca carving near Juli, known in the scientific literature as Altarani, is very popular in the mystic travel business. This impressive carving is part of a well-known tradition in Inca Empire religion. However, our New Age colleagues have a far more interesting take on this carving. It is famous as a "vortex" or special place in New Age religion and part of a "ceremony of Acceleration [that] will open your connection to the 7 portals of Ascension energy and bring you to the steps of the Galactic Stairway."[35] The more prosaic yet equally fascinating interpretation of the site by scholars is rejected for vastly more fantastic hypotheses (it is admittedly difficult for science to compete with metaphysical accelerations and portals to other worlds). Thousands of people visit Altarani each year. It is called Aramu Muru and described as "an inter-dimensional gateway and where the seeds of all existence originated."[36] Another website tells us that:

> Another legend tells of the time when the Spanish Conquistadors arrived in Peru, and looted gold and precious stones from the Inca tribes—and one Incan priest of the temple of the seven rays named Aramu Maru fled from his temple with a sacred golden disk known as The Key of the Gods of the Seven Rays. He hid in the mountains of Hayu Marca. He eventually came upon the doorway which was being watched by shaman priests. He showed them the key of the gods and a ritual was performed with the conclusion of a magical occurrence initiated by the golden disk which opened the portal, and according to the legend blue light did emanate from a tunnel inside. The priest Aramu Maru handed the golden disk to the shaman and then passed through the portal never to be seen again.[37]

Most of the alternative literature contains the common theme of a great conspiracy: mainstream science wants to suppress evidence of humanity's antiquity or evidence of extraterrestrial influence, but a few brave people are willing to risk their careers to bring this conspiracy to light. A Web site for a New Age–oriented travel company in Sedona, Arizona, says, "There are now a few brave researchers, who are willing to face the rejection of the mainstream academics and are publishing the suppressed evidence supporting the knowledge of our ancient ancestors."[41]

The fact is that virtually all mainstream scholars have little interest in suppressing information—quite the contrary, since an extraordinary discovery that overturns conventional scientific wisdom is hugely rewarding for the lucky scholar who makes it. However, it is true that at times we scientists lose our dispassion in defending what we believe to be commonsense explanations of humanity's history. One motive is the compulsion to defend the integrity and dignity of the indigenous peoples of the Americas. Over the years, claims for extraterrestrial or other fantastic origins of the world's ancient civilizations have focused on areas with the fewest practicing professional indigenous historians and archaeologists. It is insulting to the descendants of these civilizations to suggest that their culture was insufficiently talented to produce great inventions, religions, works of art, architecture, and so forth on its own. In wealthier countries, professional scholars have the time and resources to critically examine and destroy fantastic claims. In every instance where claims of extraterrestrial or transoceanic origins have been made and examined, they have either been dismissed with the evidence at hand or have been relegated to the category of subjective interpretation that is neither provable nor falsifiable.

In other words, it is somewhat easy to make unsupported claims of extraterrestrial or extracontinental influence in cultures that are underdeveloped because those with the most passion to refute such claims do not have the financial resources to conduct research and publish the results in a vigorous manner, as scholars from richer countries do. Fortunately, in the last generation, a number of highly trained professional Bolivian, Peruvian, and foreign scholars have worked in the Titicaca region. These researchers have produced a strong body of evidence that easily refutes the fantastic claims and demonstrates how indigenous peoples themselves were responsible for great cultural achievements. In the end, science gives us that truly fantastic story of how humble hunters and gatherers slowly but indefatigably built with their own hands the great civilizations of the ancient Americas, rivaling or even surpassing in some ways those of the ancient Western world. . With the next chapter we enter in world of science, a world where historical facts and observations become more fascinating than all of the legends combined.

410612 E _____ X _____ _____

ov. So. AM. 1956 __X__ . Venez 1969_____ . WGS _____

opográfica: Pampa_____ . Montículo_____ . Qda. Fondo_____ . Qda. Ladera_____

 base_____ . C. Ladera_____ . C. Cumbre_____ . C. Peñón_____ . (Orilla Río) derecho

 Lago/laguna_____ . Corte Río_____ . Otra_____

ero_____ . moderado_____ . suave __X__

cales _____

de la tierra __cultivo y pastoreo__

gua más cercana __Río Cala Cala a 20 m__

centamiento moderno __No__

l sitio __50 x 20 m__

el material superficial Baja_____ . Mod_____ . Alta_____ . Muy Alta_____

ríticos:
nta de proyectiles: ≃ 10, de chert, cuarcita ; _____ Arc_____ y Fri___ítivo_____

ramientas agrícolas: __No__

cas: de obsidiana, basalto, chert, w_____

os:

rámicas:
cripción general: fragm Collao e Inca con _____ crema

stani)

lotos:
llo 56 . nos. 01 , punta y lascas en _____ r
llo ___ . nos. _____

n general del sitio incluyendo arquitectura, tumbas, ubicación, relación a otros sitios, ocupaciones
ombres de informantes, etc. (sigue al reverso si es necesario):

pamento y taller al aire libre, ubicado en una elevación s___
, ambos sitios comparten el área inundable del pequeño riac___
hacia el río Cala Cala.
to, posiblemente hay huellas de ceniza en la zona erosion___
cala cala donde hay mayor dispersión de lascas.

SCIENCE

The first systematic scientific work in the Titicaca region began in the nineteenth century. Prior to this time, there was a rich tradition of Western explorers and naturalists traveling the Andes in search of exotic peoples and places. Even before that, indigenous intellectuals speculated on the nature of the ruins and ancient civilizations of the region. Many of these observations were incorporated into the first written accounts by Spanish chroniclers in the sixteenth and seventeenth centuries. Serious archaeological research began in earnest in the twentieth century in Peru and Bolivia, and this tradition continues to the present day. Over the past 50 years, we have learned a tremendous amount about the ancient peoples of the Titicaca region. This scientific knowledge is even more exciting than the myths and legends—precisely because it is historically accurate and is the product of real people.

The First Peoples of the Lake Titicaca Region

Archaeological research has definitively established that the first peoples to live in the greater Titicaca region had immigrated in by at least 8000 BC and probably no earlier than 10,000 BC. These people were itinerant hunters and food gatherers who lived principally along rivers and the lake edge. They hunted wild llamas and alpacas, fished from lakes and rivers, collected wild plants throughout the region, and traded for obsidian and other goods over great distances. The people lived in small groups of no more than fifty, probably far fewer, and lived a nomadic life, following the seasons and game.

We have found hundreds of their campsites and temporary living areas. We can identify their presence by distinctive arrowheads and spear points made for hunting wild animals. Archaeological excavations in the high altiplano in the western Titicaca region have discovered these points in stratigraphic columns in caves and rockshelters. In these excavations, archaeologists are able to secure carbon for very

Opposite: Some of the oldest artifacts in the Titicaca region seen here on the archaeologist's field form.
Previous: UCLA archaeologist Colleen Zori at a newly-discovered Inca site in the Atacama desert..

A vicuña, one of the earliest camelids used by the ancient peoples of the high Andes.

precise radiometric dating. Each projectile point type (arrow or spear) is distinctive in style. Some styles are restricted to relatively short time periods, and the carbon associated with them can be dated to within less than a century. As a result, scholars such as Duccio Bonavia, Cynthia Klink, and Mark Aldenderfer have isolated narrow strata and dated the point styles to specific time periods.

The time period of the first peoples in the region is referred to as the Archaic period. The Archaic period is divided into several broad subperiods, such as Early, Middle, and Late. The Archaic ends in a transitional phase known as the Terminal Archaic, that dates from around 2500 to 2000 BC. Archaeological sites from the early time periods abound in the region. The main settlements are found along rivers and on the margins of prehistoric marshes, or *bofedales* as they are called in the local

Opposite: A rock outcrop with petroglyphs carved in antiquity.
Following page: The vast expanse of the puna near Mazo Cruz.

terminology. It is not possible to see many of the ancient *bofedales*, because the climate has changed dramatically over the last 10,000 years. But scientists using sophisticated computer models have been able to define where many bofedales would have been throughout prehistory. How do we do that? Well, we simply input topographical and geological data into program and "add water". That is, we input increased rainfall levels as determined by independent data sets, such as ice cores from glaciers. We then run these models and see where the marshes and small lakes would naturally form under the ancient conditions. Archaeological field research on the ground then is used to survey near these areas produced by the computer models. This work in fact has confirmed the existence of sites around marshes and rivers that date to the earliest periods.

Most of the settlements were small camps used by wandering groups of people. We find buried in the ground the remains of stone tools, ancient llama and alpaca bones (this was before camelids were domesticated; they were wild creatures, similar to the modern vicuña), and obsidian glass fragments brought all the way from

the Arequipa region to the northwest. Our evidence shows that the lake region was an exceptionally good place to live in those days. Sites from the Archaic period abound around the lake and its immediate environs, particularly along the rivers and next to the lake edge. Many people lived in the high mountain regions above the lake as well, the area called the puna or altiplano grasslands. This was a lifestyle based upon camelids—llamas and alpacas. This way of life continued for millennia, making it one of the most successful strategies for survival on the harsh altiplano yet documented.

The Early Civilizations, circa 1800 BC to AD 500

Something big happened in the Titicaca region in the second millennium BC. The very successful Terminal Archaic–period peoples started to change lifeways that had been successful for several millennia. In a few places, we see that the formerly mobile hunter-foragers started to move less and stay in certain places for longer periods. Crude pottery, in some cases now barely distinguishable from naturally baked clay,

A Pucara style feline head from a pottery vessel, circa AD 100.

was invented and widely used around 1600 BC. Peoples throughout the region and beyond took up this innovation and elaborated the technology over the centuries. Pottery is important not just because it is useful for storing and cooking foods but because it is heavy and not easily transportable. Archaeologists recognize that when people start to make large pots, they are also more likely to stay in one place for longer periods. The first steps in creating fully permanent villages are correlated with the invention and widespread use of pottery. Over time, a few of these villages grew in size and complexity. They would become the towns of the Titicaca region a millennium or so later.

By 1300 BC, scores of villages around the lake region boasted populations into the hundreds. These were the first places in the Titicaca region where people

Opposite: A Qaluyu style pottery vessel, circa 800- 400 BC.

One of the scores of unexplored sunken courts in the Titicaca region.

came together to live in concentrated areas and to collaborate on economic, architectural, religious, and other projects. People there made beautiful pottery and other objects and started a tradition of civilized life that continued for almost two millennia.

It was at this time that people built large terraces above plaza areas, such as the one excavated by Aimée Plourde near the town of Putina in far northern Titicaca.[42] This site, called Cachichupa, was one of a half dozen or so large sites built in the Huancané–Putina river valley in the late second millennium BC. The large terraces were most likely built at the same time, with the largest platform supporting an open area where feasting and other religious activities took place. People lived below the site in large compounds composed of smaller internal rooms.

Opposite: A Qaluyu period stela housed in the archaeological museum in Pucara.

7 9

A Pucara Period stela showing felines. This beautiful piece can be seen in the Pucara Museum.

This kind of architectural organization is a first for the region. After millennia of moving in nomadic rounds, the people built a village, with a public space for ritual and other activities, and organized themselves into distinct compounds.

It is likely that each compound was the home of a distinct social group, perhaps similar to what modern peoples of the Andes call an ayllu. Ayllus are landholding social units that provide cohesion and identity to the people. Ayllus are sometimes grouped into "high" and "low" ones, giving a classic Andean duality to the social structure. In this sense, high and low do not refer to good or bad or differential status, but rather invoke a whole system of oppositions, such as male and female, earth and water, and so forth. For the Westerner, this is a difficult if not impenetrable social structure. But for Andean peoples, it is second nature. We do not know if this system began as early as the second millennium BC, but we can say that some sort of social organizing principle indeed began at this time, and this most likely was a prototype for the ayllu system so prevalent in the Andes today.

It was around this time that Titicaca-region peoples developed a set of architectural principles that would dominate their social and physical world for almost 1,500 years. The Kalasasaya complex is composed of three basic elements: a square or slightly trapezoidal sunken court built partially into the ground, an enclosure wall, and an elevated area or pyramid. The sunken court was always faced with stone and was a few meters deep. Sunken courts in the Titicaca area have antecedents throughout the central Andes, both on the coast and in the highlands, that go back to the third millennium BC. Sunken courts were extraordinarily powerful places where ritual and political life played out in villages. There is no real functional reason to build elaborate buildings with monoliths, fancy plastered walls, niches, and other design features. The courts were centers of communal life, where great feasts and other events occurred. One of the first documented sunken courts in the entire Titicaca region was discovered in the Pucara Valley in the far northwest of the region by UCLA archaeologist Amanda Cohen.[43] Another, seen in the photograph on page 83, was discovered by Adán Umire and his team during our archaeological survey in the northern Titicaca region near Lake Arapa. The photograph shows a modern corral that covers the early court complex, while the depression represents an ancient court that has since filled in with natural alluvium.

It is likely that each of the sunken courts had stone stelae or monoliths inside, at least by the beginning of the first millennium BC. Stelae were central to these cultures and were the focus of ethnic identity and political life. Stelae were carved in sandstone, basalt, andesite, limestone and virtually any kind of rock. Some reached up to four meters high. Most of the stelae were not carved, but some of the most spectacular have elaborate carvings, particularly frogs, fish, serpents, human faces, pumas and geometric designs.

The custom spread throughout the Titicaca region, from the far north to at least the great desert plains around the Carangas area in the south. The enclosures are almost always made of low stone walls and were designed to hold a number of people on or near the summit of the low pyramid. While the sunken courts in this early period may have held a few dozen people at most, the enclosures were designed to hold many more, most likely all the people in each village.

The pyramids were originally very low mounds that grew in size over time. Early on, the pyramids were usually just low hills. In many cases, they were just natural hills that were modified to look like pyramids. Very few of these low pyramids have been scientifically excavated. Most now have few or no remains on the surface. We can guess, however, that they had some kind of building at the top. On the coast of Peru, early sites have adobe structures on top of pyramids that clearly were used for ritual and political events. Excavations at sites such as Aspero on the north coast of Peru indicate that elaborate ceremonies took place on the pyramid tops. Archaeologists have discovered burned floors from burning rituals and artifact offerings such as feathers, fruit-tree branches, figurines, and pigments.[44] It is likely that similar ceremonies took place on top of Titicaca-area pyramids, as well as in small stone and adobe buildings built by the community for religious observances.

These three architectural elements—sunken courts, enclosures, and raised areas or pyramids—were essential in the political and religious life of the people of this early period. One can imagine the kinds of ceremonies and performances that these architectural features evoked and orchestrated in villages. People would gather around the village, perhaps feast in the enclosures, then a select few elders would move to the sunken courts. Like the great kivas in the American Southwest among the Ancestral Pueblo peoples, the courts would have been used for various kinds of ceremonies that we are just beginning to understand. Finally, we can imagine even more elaborate and restricted ceremonies on the pyramids themselves, where elders or all household heads gathered to reinforce the religious, social, and other cultural bonds of the community. Around 1300 to 800 BC, the entire Titicaca region was full of small temples on hills surrounding the lake. There was no central government or any kind of political unity at this time. People most likely identified with their smaller home community which in turn was ideologically identified through the art and architecture. Each monolith would have served to both represent a village or multi-village coalition while also expressing a pan regional religion that all could identify with. It would have been similar to Medieval Europe with scores of independent political units--kingdoms both large and small--all adopting versions of Christianity. The region would have been an amazing place to visit, with thousands of small temples surrounded by bustling, thriving villages.

ove: An early sunken court in the northern Titicaca Basin near the Putina River.
lowing pages: The town and site of Pukara, in the far northern Titicaca Basin.

One of the principal sunken courts at Pucara.

A closer view of one of the sunken courts at Pucara.

Pucara

The Kalasasaya complex of courts, enclosures, and pyramids was elaborated on a large scale at the site of Pucara, located about 50 kilometers north of Juliaca on the road to Cusco. Pucara is one of the most important sites in ancient Peru. People first moved to Pucara around 1400 BC and continued to live there for at least 1,700 more years. The site is large, around 150 hectares at its peak around AD 200 (A hectare is roughly the size of two American football fields placed side by side). The main architectural feature of Pucara is a series of large terraces that lead up to a flat area. This flat area has two sunken courts, with a third unexcavated one in the same group. The sunken courts are large—larger than any other built in the Titicaca region up to this time. The biggest court measures circa 16 by 16 meters in size and is a bit over two meters deep.[45] The court is built with large cut slabs set upright, a typical pattern for this period.

In front of the large terraced construction is an area where people lived in what was otherwise a regular village. There is a series of mounds that most likely had sunken courts as well. Likewise, directly south of this area are at least three other mounds with evidence of sunken courts. Residential areas are found near and on these mound areas, and the archaeological remains of the settlement are found toward the modern road. Pucara is not a planned site like the later Tiwanaku capital or the Inca-period urban sites that dot the Titicaca region. Pucara is in fact a very large concentration of houses built around a number of fancy sunken courts. The sunken courts vary from very large ones at the top of the main mound to smaller courts seen on the low mounds to the east. To get some perspective, the town of Pucara in the second century AD was about the size of fourteenth-century London.

There is good evidence that the courts were used for large-scale feasts, perhaps military displays, and even human sacrifice, something like miniature versions of the Roman Coliseum. Michigan archaeologist Sergio Chávez documented the existence of 100 human mandible and skull parts from a single area in the collections of the excavations conducted by the late great archaeologist Alfred Kidder II. Kidder most

Above: The interior of the Pucara Museum highlighting the famous "Decapitator Stela".
Following: Scenes from the Pucara Museum courtyard.

likely excavated the remains of war captives buried, or reburied, during a politically important ceremony. Near this area, archaeologist Elizabeth Klarich discovered deep garbage deposits associated with open areas in front of the main courts. She also discovered the remains of feasting activities.[46] In other words, the site has three very large courts and a number of smaller ones, all of which may have functioned at the same time to host feasts, ceremonies, and other rites performed by all members of the community. One can imagine living in Pucara in the second century AD. Spreading over an area the size of late medieval London, the site was a vast and bustling metropolis. The base of the hill all the way to the river was full of adobe buildings, where most people lived. Above this residential area were the impressive stone-faced temples, with high terrace walls that led to open spaces. It would have

The interior of the Taraco Museum

been a dramatic and exciting place to be. In fact, it was one of the largest and most sophisticated towns in all of Peru and Bolivia at the time, a highly charged religious and political town that buzzed with activity, 365 days a year.

Pucara art is famous, particularly the monoliths. The National Institute of Culture, under the direction of Rolando Paredes and Chela Fattorini, rebuilt the museum near the site at the edge of the town of Pucara. The museum exhibits beautiful examples of monolithic stone sculpture and pottery. Early Pucara or Qaluyu stelae depict animals such as frogs, fish, and snakes. Most of these monoliths were found on the site of Pucara itself. They were most likely originally found in the sunken courts that were built over the site area and functioned for centuries as ritual centers. It is also likely that many of the stelae at Pucara were captured huacas,

Opposite: A Pucara period sculpture.
Following: Two Qaluyu period stelae from the Taraco Museum.

or symbolic objects, from other villages. Huacas are a peculiarly Andean concept; a material object or natural place represents the soul or "vitality" of a people. Huacas can be springs, rock outcrops, carved rocks, special objects, and of course stelae. The town and ancient archaeological site of Taraco, some 50 kilometers from Pucara, had a number of monoliths that may have been carried off to Pucara. Like the capture of the Arapa stela by Tiwanaku (described below), the movement of the monuments of conquered foes was a common practice in the ancient world. Pucara is full of monoliths—a fact that highlights just how important the site was in the greater Lake Titicaca region 2,000 years ago.

Taraco

Until recently, the town of Taraco and the archaeological remains beneath it were known mainly for the beautiful monoliths found there, such as those seen in the local museum. The small museum houses some of the greatest pieces of cut-stone art in the ancient world and certainly deserves a visit if you are in the area. Recent research reveals that the ancient site of Taraco in fact was a huge town that rivaled Pucara and Tiwanaku in size and importance between 500 BC and AD 300. (Taraco is located in the northern Titicaca Basin in Peru and should not be confused with the Taraco Peninsula in the south in Bolivia).

The ancient town of Taraco is actually composed of about a dozen large and small mounds scattered on each side of the Ramis River. The main mound is under the modern town of Taraco and covers around 50 hectares up to the river and almost to the modern road. Throughout the northern Titicaca region are the remains of an extensive culture dating back to the first and second millennia. Excavations near the plaza show that people had settled in permanent villages in Taraco by at least 1400 BC, about the same time as settlement at Cachichupa in the Putina area and Pucara, described above. The villages rested over earlier Archaic hunting–fishing camps that go back several millennia more. Around 500 BC, Taraco grew in size and importance. By the first centuries of the first millennium AD, the settlement was one of the most

Opposite: Excavations in the mound in the town of Taraco, Puno.

9 7

powerful centers in the Titicaca region, rivaled only by Pucara.

In 2004 Puno archaeologist Cecilia Chávez uncovered one of the greatest discoveries in the archaeology of the Andes in many years near the town of Taraco; she found an 8-meter-high pyramid built after Pucara times. This site is located about a kilometer from the modern town and had an adobe pyramid with a ramp dating to the middle of the first millennium AD. Below this level were the remains of earlier pyramids belonging to the Pucara and Late Qaluyu periods. Other mounds around Taraco belonged to this complex of pyramids and villages, which survived for several hundred years after the Pucara period. The origins of these people, known as the Huaña culture, remain a mystery. The only known contemporary groups that had adobe pyramids were on the coast of Peru. Ancient coastal cities such Cajamarquilla and Pachacamac, located near Lima, had ramped structures built with adobe, but this architectural technique had never been documented in the Titicaca region before. Since 2004 Chávez and her colleagues have found more adobe constructions in the ancient Taraco complex, but the mystery indeed remains: Who were these people who started building pyramids in "coastal" styles? Where did they come from and how did they come to Taraco? Were they Taraceños who adopted "foreign" architecture and religion? Were the adobe ramps imitations of Tiwanaku stone types? Were they migrants who took advantage of the political turmoil of the post-Pucara periods in the region?

Around AD 200 there was a major catastrophe at Taraco. Archaeological excavations by UCLA archaeologist Abby Levine, Chávez and the author tell us there was a major burning of at least one very large area of the town. This area housed relatively high-status people. The evidence shows that their houses were burned to the ground, including the posts that held up the roofs. After this event, Taraco ceased to create or import fancy pottery and commodities such as obsidian glass. The town of Taraco, which had survived for centuries as a major regional power, ceased to be significant. It is likely there was a bloody competition between Taraco and Pucara, and the latter won this fight and went on for a century or two more as the dominant political center in the region. By the end of the fourth century AD, however, Pucara itself had collapsed, and the people who built the adobe pyramids first discovered by Cecilia Chávez dominated the region for the next two or three centuries.

Chiripa

Located on the far south of the lake edge in modern Bolivia, the site of Chiripa on the Taraco Peninsula is another famous early village in the Titicaca region. Excavations by Gregorio Cordero in the 1950s and 1970s discovered an early sunken court that archaeologist Karen Mohr Chávez recognized as one of the earliest such structures in the Titicaca region.[47] The building is approximately 22 x 23 meters in size and was built 1.5 meters into the ground. William Conklin and Michael Moseley reconstructed the architecture of this complex, showing a series of structures around a central plaza.[48] Karen Chávez described the buildings as residential and as storage structures with elaborate decorations, including painted walls and red washes, interior yellow clay floors, decorative niches, and double-jamb doorways with step frets.

Below the mound at Chiripa are several terraces that held houses and other special buildings. While almost never reported until Christine Hastorf and her team conducted their research over the last 15 years, these household terraces indicate that Chiripa was, in fact, not an isolated "temple" site but a more complicated village complex of elite houses, community constructions in the form of elaborate political and religious ceremonial architecture, and substantial regular housing or storage areas surrounding the ceremonial core.

We used to think that Chiripa was a special site in the region during this early time period. In the last decade or so of research, we have discovered dozens of sites like Chiripa. In fact, scores of sunken court sites and temples from the first half of the first millennium BC have been found in the Titicaca region. We now know that this kind of site was quite common throughout the area, like the earlier phases at Pucara. These sites were the locations of the first complex villages that developed during the emergence of civilization in the Titicaca area. Small villages emerged as important political nodes throughout the region. It was in reference to this time that we can first speak of "politics" on a regional scale. Each site with a sunken court represented a politically important village or town where economic and religious activity took place. These activities were centered on the sunken courts and included feasting, work-related rituals, distribution of precious and exotic goods, and possibly marriages and other important social activities. We can say that civilization, as is commonly understood to mean the development of complex social, political, and economic institutions, truly emerged during this time and that Chiripa and scores of other sites in the Titicaca region represent this incredible cultural development. Chiripa has become an important tourist destination on the Bolivian side, well worth the few hours' visit by the adventurous traveler.

Opposite: A Tiwanaku style pottery kero found in Moquegua, Peru.

The Kalasasaya or Great Enclosure at the ancient city of Tiwanaku.

The First Great City in the Titicaca Region: Tiwanaku

The collapse of the northern Titicaca civilizations of Pucara and Taraco was complete by around AD 400 and probably a bit earlier. The north witnessed a new era in which people dispersed from the large towns into a number of villages and hamlets. It was also in this time that new peoples most likely migrated into the area, possibly from the coast. As noted above, this was the time in which the adobe pyramids were built in the north. In effect, the great civilizations of the northern Titicaca region were collapsing, though the people themselves were still there. It is important to understand that there are two kinds of civilizational collapse. One is very severe—a loss of population through death or migration. The second is a political breakdown

The semi-subterranean sunken court at Tiwanaku.

that does not result in population loss but where the centers of art, religion, and so forth fade away. The second type is vastly more common in history. This is what happened in the northern Titicaca region in the fourth to seventh centuries of this era. First Taraco fell. A couple of centuries later, Pucara collapsed as well. People dispersed to hamlets and villages away from the formerly great town, but they were still nearby living and working in the region.[49] It was also during this time that immigrants into the region probably took advantage of the political chaos to settle with their new pyramids.

While the people in the Taraco area were dispersing across the region and new immigrants were building their enigmatic adobe pyramids, the people of Tiwanaku were just beginning to build what would become a sophisticated kingdom,

Opposite: Tenoned heads in the sunken court at Tiwanaku.

one of the most advanced civilizations of the ancient world. From at least 2,200 years ago to the late seventh century, Tiwanaku was a regional center, about the size of Pucara at its height. From the eighth to the eleventh century AD, Tiwanaku was one of the great capitals of the ancient world, projecting its influence over an area the size of California. Around the end of the tenth or beginning of the eleventh century, Tiwanaku started a century-long decline as a regional power, ultimately converting into a mysterious ruin by the time the Incas arrived in the late fifteenth century.

Even as early as Inca times, the city held a special place in the Andean consciousness. In 1653 the Spanish historian and naturalist Bernabé Cobo related the story of the Inca emperor Pachacuti's impression of Tiwanaku during his campaign in Collasuyu: "Pachacuti saw the magnificent buildings of Tiaguanaco [an alternative spelling for Tiwanaku], and the stonework of these structures amazed him because he had never seen that type of building before; and he commanded that his men should carefully observe and take note of that building method, because he wanted the construction projects in Cusco to be of that same type of workmanship."

These words reinforce the observation that the so-called Inca-style masonry of Cusco is found on earlier sites in the Titicaca region. The origin of Cusco-style Inca stonecutting has been a mystery for some time. Without question, the Inca were the undisputed masters of this technique. But it is likely that they imported this style from the Titicaca region. We have sites such as Tanka Tanka in the far southern Peruvian territory near the Bolivian border with classic Inca-style masonry in a decidedly pre-Inca site. Likewise, Tiwanaku itself and Pucara both have stone carving that is similar in style to and centuries older than the Inca buildings. These observations, and many more, indicate to us that the so-called Inca style actually predates the Inca period and was most certainly invented before the Empire. It is quite possible that this stoneworking technique was first invented in the Titicaca basin.

The capital of the Tiwanaku state was built over a long period. It is located on the Bolivian altiplano, in the middle of the Tiwanaku Valley, approximately 20 kilometers from the lake edge. At its height, around AD 750 to 900, Tiwanaku was a massive concentration of peoples living and working around an impressive architectural core of pyramids, palaces, streets, and state buildings. It was home to a powerful elite who built palaces and had huge stone stelae carved in their honor. Surrounding the core of the capital was an urban settlement of artisans, laborers, and farmers who lived in adobe structures up and down the valley.

The vast, planned urban capital sprawled over the altiplano landscape in this rich valley. The city was four to six square kilometers in area, with a population ranging from 30,000 to 60,000.[50] To put this in perspective, London in the sixteenth century was about the same size. The suburban valley area between Tiwanaku and the lake was also heavily populated during the height of the city. The combined population of these settlements and the capital would have been quite substantial in the ninth and tenth centuries AD. Tiwanaku and its immediate environs represent the greatest concentration of people in the Andes south of Cusco prior to the Spanish conquest in the sixteenth century.

As a capital city of what archaeologists call an expansive archaic state, Tiwanaku was more than a mere urban concentration of artisans, commoners, and

Opposite: Tiwanaku incense burner from the Puno area.

political elite. Tiwanaku served as the architectural representation of the power of a state with influence over a vast area in the south-central Andes, although this influence was highly varied across the political landscape. A large, terraced, artificial-stone-faced pyramid in the urban core of the site dominates the Tiwanaku capital. Known as the Akapana, this construction measures 197 x 257 meters at its base and is 16.5 meters high. Six stone-faced terraces outlined the hill. The Akapana was shaped like a half Andean cross with a cross-shaped sunken court on its top.

The Akapana is a huge construction and was most certainly one of the principal political and sacred "public" areas in the capital. Significantly, there were "distinctly secular structures" built at the top of the pyramid that the University of Chicago archaeologist Alan Kolata interprets as the houses of a noble class. We know that people lived there because archaeologists have found a lot of common refuse in the buried garbage dumps near the house foundations. The rectangular houses were built with finely cut stones and faced inward toward a patio area, not unlike the much smaller and earlier constructions at Chiripa, Pucara, Cachichupa and other earlier

The backside of the Puerta del Sol in Tiwanaku.

sites in the region. Oswaldo Rivera, the former director of the Bolivian Institute of Archaeology, also discovered buildings on the lower terraces, indicating that much of the Akapana housed a noble or priestly class. National Geographic Society explorer Johan Reinhard interprets the Akapana as an artificial sacred mountain—an interpretation with which I agree. In other words, a group of nobles at Tiwanaku lived on the artificial sacred mountain of the capital. The ability to live on the most precious ground in a city is a very profound political and social statement about a person's status in society. It is also significant that the shape of the Akapana is reproduced throughout Tiwanaku art and architecture, attesting to the importance of this motif.

Adjacent to the north face of the Akapana is a large, walled enclosure known as the Kalasasaya. The Kalasasaya is almost square, measuring 120 x 130 meters, and is slightly elevated above the ground surface. There is also a sunken court in the complex, along with a series of buildings of unknown function. The walls of the Kalasasaya are built with massive, upright stone blocks and smaller shaped stones, giving the enclosure a monumental appearance. Monolithic stone sculptures, such as the Bennett and Ponce stelae, have been found in the Kalasasaya. It is likely that they were placed there during the height of the capital. The Kalasasaya was cardinally oriented, and there may have been some astronomical, specifically equinoctial, alignments to the architecture. A staircase on the east provides access to this impressive architectural complex. Even with this staircase, however, the architectural plan of the Kalasasaya restricts access to the interior. Archaeologists believe that the nature of access to large spaces in urban areas is extremely significant. The degree to which access is restricted is the degree to which it is controlled by a small group of people. The degree to which it is open—say Central Park in New York—is the degree to which there is less overt social and political control in a society. The Kalasasaya was a highly restricted space in the center of one of the great cities of the ancient world. It functioned as a locus for religious and political ritual, as suggested by the large and open area. It also housed possible storage structures that may have contained incredibly important objects, maybe even the mummies of the dead rulers of Tiwanaku.

Below the Kalasasaya is the semi-subterranean sunken court. This court is a stone-lined open building that is slightly trapezoidal, measuring approximately 26 x 28 meters on its sides. Like earlier counterparts in centuries past, the court at Tiwanaku was built partially below the ground surface. As in the Kalasasaya, stelae were found in the court. Along with the Akapana and Kalasasaya, the sunken court formed a political and religious complex used for important state rituals promoting the state power vested in the nobility of Tiwanaku.[51] The sunken court has carved stone heads built into and along the sides of the walls.

The court is reconstructed, but this work from the 1970s appears to be a reasonably faithful reconstruction of the original architecture. I agree with other scholars and view the heads as representations of captured huacas of various villages

Opposite: Blocks from Tiwanaku showing the use of metal clamps.

and subject polities of the Tiwanaku state at its height, probably contemporary with the carving of the Bennett and Ponce stelae, two huge monoliths found at the site.[52] It is significant that the heads were placed in the sunken court below the Kalasasaya in a visible location. Furthermore, one of the most striking characteristics of the carved heads is their variability in style. This variability tells us that the carvings probably represent trophy heads of individual people, as depicted occasionally on Pucara and Tiwanaku art. Another interpretation is that they were symbols of particular villages or towns captured by Tiwanaku armies. In this sense the heads would be analogous to the captured flags of countries or even military units in modern war. The victor captures symbols of the enemy and displays them in one of the most important architectural centers of their city.

In my view and that of many other archaeologists, the sunken court and the Kalasasaya housed captured stelae that, as huacas from defeated enemies, also represented incorporated towns, villages or other territories of this early empire. One of the most interesting discoveries in Titicaca-area archaeology was the

identification by Sergio Chávez of the Arapa stela as the complementary half of the Thunderbolt stela found in Tiwanaku.[53] The Arapa stela is from the town of the same name, about 225 kilometers from Tiwanaku in the northern Titicaca region. The stela was broken and about half of it was moved to Tiwanaku by boat or by a foot march down the lake edge. This broken half was placed in the ceremonial area of the city. The decoration of the stela is a few centuries earlier than the rise of Tiwanaku as a large city. This date is well established, based upon stylistic comparisons from other sites in the Pucara tradition. This tells us that the monolith was brought to Tiwanaku long after it was carved by the people in Arapa. Stelae have important social and political meanings for villages today, and it is likely that the Arapa stela was being used by a group of people long after it was carved as a huaca of their village.

I agree with those archaeologists who see the Arapa stela as further evidence of huaca capture, just like the tenoned heads on the sides of the sunken court. Throughout the Andes, anthropologists and historians have noted the significance of stelae to communities or political groups. The capture of such symbols therefore has profound political significance. The capture of enemy symbols and their display in the victor's capital is common throughout history and prehistory for societies such as Tiwanaku. One of my favorite examples from the Western world is that of England's King Edward in his conquest of the Scottish kingdom in 1296. With the captive King John Balliol firmly held in the Tower of London, Edward advanced through Aberdeen, Banff, and Elgin to display his royal power and to have the local people acknowledge his authority. The account of this conquest as related by Ronald McNair Scott provides what I believe to be an appropriate analogy to the removal of the Arapa stela to Tiwanaku. Edward ordered the "Stone of Destiny" to be removed to London. For generations, Scottish kings had used this relic to prove that they had been granted the authority of office. Scott notes, "The plunder of this sacred relic and the royal regalia which he had already removed from Edinburgh castle were arrogant signals to all in Scotland that henceforth their country was not a kingdom but a dependent part of England." Such a profound symbolic and political message was sent each time Tiwanaku people captured another area and removed its huacas to Tiwanaku itself.[54]

A little less than a kilometer to the southwest of the Akapana is the building complex known as the Pumapunku. The Pumapunku (which literally means "door [or gate] of the puma in Aymara") is now a mound that once housed elaborate stone and adobe buildings. Subterranean canals were constructed under the Pumapunku as well, indicating that the entire complex was planned and constructed at one period. There are two sets of stairs on the east and west sides of the Pumapunku, much like at the Akapana. In fact, during the height of the city, these two incredible buildings would have dominated the architectural core of the city. John Janusek has pointed out that the architecture of the Pumapunku allows for some of the most dramatic views of the Ccapia Mountains to the northwest and the iconic Illimani Mountain beyond La Paz to the east. It is most certain that mountain worship, or at least mountain viewing, was an integral part of the architectural planning of buildings such as the Pumapunku.

Excavations by archaeologists from the University of Chicago have discovered elaborate decorative sculpture and painting in the Pumapunku. The project director describes the eastern court as having elaborate carved door jambs, lintels, sculptures, and the like. He even suggests that this was the original location of the beautiful Puerta del Sol, now found in the Kalasasaya.[55] The cut masonry that graced the exterior of the Pumapunku is unrivaled at the city. Pumapunku was the second most important monument at Tiwanaku after the Akapana, if considered in terms of labor investment, artistic effort, workmanship, and size.

The Putuni is located directly to the west of the Kalasasaya and is the spatial counterpart to the semi-subterranean court to the east. The Putuni, in Kolata's words, is a "Palace of the Lords." He accurately notes that the building stands out from other architecture on the site, being characterized by a slightly elevated platform with a sunken court or plaza area. The Putuni was most likely housing for the nobility of Tiwanaku. It may have been a temple as well, though our research on this important building is still in its infancy. The fact that it is attached to the Kalasasaya enclosure is significant. As a palace for the most elite members of Tiwanaku society, the Putuni has some of the finest architecture in the ancient Andes.

The Island of the Sun photographed from the village of Yumani to the north, with the celebrated travel professional Daniel Salazar in the foreground. The island was an early territory of the Tiwanaku State.

Janusek describes the elaborate stone washbasins set into the floors of the Putuni and nearby Kherikala compounds.[56] In fact, these elite residences had some of the earliest formal bathing areas and underground plumbing in the Andes, a truly monumental feat of engineering. Janusek goes on to describe how the Putuni and Kherikala were razed in the late eighth or early ninth century and a huge new palace area was built to house perhaps a new dynasty. This construction involved elaborate feasts and sacrifices of animals and occasionally even human beings of all ages, both men and women. They were similar to the offerings found at the base of the Akapana, also placed there at the time of a great monumental building project. One can imagine the scene of this event, a once-in-a-lifetime experience for everyone there, with the city filled with visitors from around the entire southern Andes.

East of the semi-subterranean temple is the area known as Kantatayita. Little systematic work has been published on this sector of the site, but it is known to have buildings similar to the Putuni. Huge blocks are found on the surface today, and what is most likely an architectural model carved in a monolithic block is found in this area. According to Carlos Ponce, a large decorated lintel was discovered in the Kantatayita area.[57] University of California–Berkeley architect Jean Pierre Protzen and University of California–Riverside art historian Stella Nair described the stunningly beautiful architrave carved on its backside.[58] These kinds of carvings would have had gold sheets pressed over the stone and held in place by nails. This kind of elaborate and beautiful architecture is found throughout Tiwanaku at places such as the Kherikala and Chunchukala.

The many architectural features we see at Tiwanaku, such as the underground sewer system and cardinally oriented layout of many of the buildings, indicate that the capital of Tiwanaku at its height was a planned city built in a relatively short period of time. Furthermore, there are many earlier phases at the site, indicating that the inhabitants rebuilt the urban center using a huge labor pool. The large stone blocks used in construction of the city's core attest the immensity of this labor pool. These blocks were massive and required an enormous and skilled group of artisans who would have had to work for years.

Work by UCLA archaeologist Alexei Vranich and his colleague Leo Benetiz demonstrate that there are a number of astronomical alignments of buildings at Tiwanaku. These scholars suggest that some of the principal objects of worship by Tiwanaku peoples were the heavens, the astronomical wonders of the preindustrial night sky. Their work shows that the Tiwanaku peoples also worshipped mountains and other major landforms in their environment. These scholars see the city of Tiwanaku as a grand visual embodiment of the Tiwanaku religion, with sight lines and building orientations being consciously created as part of the experience of pilgrims to this famous center.

Outside of this architectural core were the many houses of the common people, constructed of adobe walls over rock bases. The deterioration of the building walls, along with the grass cover after the site was abandoned, has served to obscure the vast housing areas associated with the site. An appropriate analogy for Tiwanaku would be the site of the later prehistoric city of Chan Chan, located on the coast of Peru outside the modern city of Trujillo. Like Tiwanaku, most of the buildings at Chan Chan were made of adobe. If Chan Chan were in a climate similar to Tiwanaku's, little would remain of the buildings, because heavy rains would have melted the walls. The central architectural core of the site, which is made with indestructible volcanic rock, would be preserved, while the rest of the habitation areas would have been eroded and covered with soil and grass. At Tiwanaku, virtually anytime test excavations are conducted outside the architectural core within a four-square-kilometer area, archaeological remains are found. The modern town of Tiwanaku is full of the remains of the ancient Tiwanaku people. This would be the same pattern in Chan Chan had the site been constructed in a similar environment. In other words, the nature of the architectural construction techniques and the high rainfall of the Tiwanaku area serve to obscure the monumentality of the site.

Chan Chan was about the same size as Tiwanaku, both physically and in population size, and the city was a capital of a state that controlled a large territory. Both states controlled provinces and maintained satellite communities spread over many hundreds of kilometers for economic and strategic purposes. Chan Chan had divine kingship, and the archaeological evidence from Tiwanaku suggests that it too had such a political system. Both societies had marked social classes, and both incorporated different ethnic groups, either voluntarily or otherwise, through a variety of means to create an expansive political organization of impressive proportions. The analogy to Chan Chan makes sense. The sites were Andean creations—one on the coast and one in the altiplano. Since Chan Chan is later that Tiwanaku and is in a very dry environment, we have a lot more information. But the similarities are important: Andean peoples created a number of impressive cities up in their world, and Tiwanaku stands as one of the most impressive of all.

Following page 118, top: the Island of the Sun or Titicaca, Bolivia.
Bottom, page 118: The lakeside face of the Titikala or Sacred Rock of the Inca.
Top, page 119: The Island of the Moon, or Coati, with the Cordillera Real in the background.
Bottom, page 119: The "sacred rock" of Tiwanaku, the Murokata on the Island of the Sun.

Tiwanaku on the Islands of the Sun and Moon

The islands of the Sun and Moon are famous for their Inca temples and buildings dedicated to the sun, moon, and other deities in the Inca pantheon. The Inca complex was built around 1500 and has become a popular tourist destination as well as a famous place of scientific research. Few people realize that this vast sacred complex was also a major center for the Tiwanaku kingdom, built eight centuries earlier. On the Island of the Moon, University of Illinois–Chicago archaeologist Brian Bauer located Tiwanaku pottery and intact archaeological levels under the Inca construction known as the Iñak Uyu.[59] In fact, in Inca times the Island of the Moon was part of a vast complex used by the Tiwanaku people as a great religious center as well, attracting pilgrims and merchants from around the entire south-central Andes.

Bauer and I also studied the Island of the Sun. There are at least 28 Tiwanaku sites on this much larger island, telling us that the island was one of the most densely populated and important provinces of the Tiwanaku state. Archaeologist Matthew Seddon has studied one of these sites, called Chucaripupata.[60] The site is located approximately 100 meters southeast of the Titikala, the Sacred Rock of the Incas found on the northern part of the Island of the Sun. Chucaripupata was first reported by the famous Swiss archaeologist Adolph Bandelier in 1910, during his research on the islands.[61] He described the site as an "irregular quadrangle . . . platform lined by walls and surrounded by lower terraces on three sides, whereas in the northeast it abuts against a higher plane on the flanks of Muro-Kato." Murokata is a large rocky crag east of the site that is similar to the Titikala rock in appearance. It dominates the landscape of the entire area and towers above Chucaripupata.

A series of well-made terraces is found on the northern and southern sides of the Chucaripupata platform, descending down the original ridge. No terraces are located on the western, or lake-edge, portion of the site because the terrain is too steep. At both the northern and southern areas of the site, the first terrace down from the upper platform is specially constructed. This system of walls forms a first terrace at either side of the site that is connected architecturally with the upper

platform. Below each of these descends a series of additional terraces, about ten in all, built down each slope, that are not as finely made as the first terrace.

According to Seddon, the site is comprised of a walled upper platform and descending lower terraces as originally described by Bandelier. The upper platform is approximately 60 x 60 meters, forming an irregular square. The upper platform has a slight slope running from the middle to either side, with a drop in altitude of about 1.5 meters from the middle of the platform to the northern and southern edges. As Bandelier noted, this platform area may originally have been level. Bedrock is visible on the surface at the lake-edge portion of the platform, indicating that the architects cut into solid rock to create the structure. This would have made a stunning view from the lake edge.

Scientific research, including excavations by Seddon and architectural work by the celebrated Bolivian architect Javier Escalante, tells us that there was a major set of buildings on the site, including a huge double-faced wall that may have separated sacred from nonsacred space. The high quality of pottery and other artifacts at the site indicates that Chucaripupata was an important ritual area with a number of houses located on the lower terraces. Seddon interprets the site as a major Tiwanaku ritual center maintained at the height of the Tiwanaku state. His work indicates that Tiwanaku controlled the entire island and that the Sacred Rock, the famous pilgrimage destination in the Inca Empire, was also a major ritual center in Tiwanaku times. This research leaves virtually no doubt that the original builders of the famous ritual center on the islands of the Sun and Moon were the Tiwanaku peoples who built this many centuries before than the Inca. While the Inca installations were described in detail by Spanish chroniclers, only scientific archaeology can help us understand the earlier prehistoric periods. What this work tells us is that indeed the Tiwanaku peoples created many of the institutions seen centuries later in the Inca Empire.

The location of Chucaripupata relative to the Murokata rock is similar to the location of the Inca temple relative to the Sacred Rock. I believe that the Murokata rock was the Sacred Rock of the Tiwanaku peoples and that it functioned like the

Titikala for the Inca. We can imagine a temple on Chucaripupata with rituals taking place on this earlier Sacred Rock. It is also significant that the Murokata is actually higher than the Titikala. We can speculate that Tiwanaku peoples first adopted the Murokata as their sacred huaca and that Inca peoples came in and chose the nearby Titikala for similar reasons. Perhaps the Incas had to distinguish themselves from the Tiwanaku peoples and simply had to find another huaca. Perhaps the Inca preferred the northeastern face of the Titikala to the more northerly face of the Murokata. Whatever the reason, the Murokata affords a perfect view of each shore looming above the temple area and would have been a spectacular location for state ritual. The sacred status of the island goes back to at least the eighth century AD, created by the ancestors of the Aymara who built the city of Tiwanaku and later influenced the nascent Inca Empire, much like the ancient Greeks greatly influenced the later Roman Empire.

Other islands

The Tiwanaku people also set up religious centers on smaller islands. In the south, the island of Pariti has produced some spectacular finds. In the north, the island of Amantaní has a sunken court in a Tiwanaku or even earlier style. The small island of Tikonata is particularly interesting. The community members discovered a number of mummies and Tiwanaku ceremonial objects. It is clear that this island was a major ritual location in the Tiwanaku empire. The island today has a comfortable hostel, museum and guided tours. This is a marvelous place where visitors can experience one of the principal sacred islands in lake Titicaca.

Why did Tiwanaku collapse?

Tiwanaku culture survived for several centuries, peaking around AD 850–900. Troubles in the Tiwanaku orbit began around the mid-tenth century, beginning with a gradual collapse of Tiwanaku influence in their colonial holdings. In the Moquegua Valley, located more than 100 kilometers to the west of Lake Titicaca, the beginning of the Chiribaya culture starts around AD 950—probably earlier.[62] Chiribaya developed after Tiwanaku collapsed. The beginning of the Chiribaya culture therefore dates the end of Tiwanaku influence in their provincial areas. In the Moquegua region at least, Tiwanaku influence had ended by the end of the millennium, fully a century earlier than in the core territory. We see the same date for the end of Tiwanaku to the south of Moquegua. In the Azapa Valley in far northern Chile, Tiwanaku influence appears to have faded at about the same time or even earlier than in the Moquegua Valley. Other areas outside the Titicaca region, such as Arequipa and Cochabamba, also seemed to fall outside the Tiwanaku orbit no later than the tenth century AD.

Scientific research shows us that there was a gradual, centuries-long retraction of Tiwanaku influence as a function of distance from the core territory. Paul Goldstein, an archaeologist from the University of California–San Diego, argues that the collapse of Tiwanaku influence in Moquegua, as represented by the provincial capital at the site of Omo, was accompanied by a violent episode in the 900s: "The downfall of the system came from within. All indications suggest that the sudden and deliberate destruction of the Omo site in the tenth century came at the hands of rebellious Tiwanaku provincials, rather than any outside agent."[63] The intentional destruction of the site is certainly a very important piece of archaeological evidence and indicates that the end of Tiwanaku may have been the result of some kind of violent internal rebellion or external attack. In this view, Tiwanaku was a conquest state that lost its ability to control competitors in a protracted military confrontation with a group of ever-growing enemies in its periphery.

One famous example of this military competition is seen in Moquegua at the magnificent site of Cerro Baúl. Cerro Baúl was the main settlement of the Wari peoples, who created a great civilization about the same time as Tiwanaku. The capital of Wari is found in the central highlands, near the modern town of Ayacucho. Wari's influence extended throughout the central Andes into the northern coast of Peru. Cerro Baúl is located on a famously defensive massif—once aptly described by University of Florida archaeologist Michael Moseley as the "Masada of the Andes"—that provides the highest level of protection available in any premodern settlement. Adjacent to Cerro Baúl is the site of Cerro Mejia, also a Wari-affiliated site. Surrounding Baúl is a series of Tiwanaku sites that were, for all intents and purposes, contemporary with the Wari town on the summit above.

The summit of Cerro Baúl was used for many purposes, including large ritual events. Moseley and his colleagues Donna Nash and Ryan Williams of Chicago's Field Museum of Natural History discovered smashed drinking vessels at the top, indicating that there was traditional Andean feasting going on at least 1,200 years ago. There are also some Tiwanaku pottery fragments and, according to Nash and Williams, a Tiwanaku sector on Cerro Baúl. This evidence proves that this was a place where Tiwanaku and Wari peoples met, drank, and most likely negotiated with each other. As Moseley and his colleagues say, Cerro Baúl was an "embassy-like delegation of nobles and attendant personnel that endured for centuries."[64] Cerro Baúl, in fact, is the only site outside the Titicaca region south of Arequipa where the two great civilizations of Wari and Tiwanaku interacted on a regular basis.

Cerro Baúl was also a defensive site that served to keep its Wari occupants safe from the surrounding Tiwanaku settlers. The Tiwanaku peoples did not need defensive locations in Moquegua, since they greatly outnumbered the Wari contingent. It is not a contradiction for people to be both adversaries and trading partners. In fact, competing political groups rarely have actual battles for more than a mere fraction of time. It is very common in the historical literature to see a cooperative "live and let live" philosophy among states, even among adversaries. It is also true that this norm is occasionally punctured by outbursts of violence. These outbursts can indeed have enormous political and other consequences, but they are actually quite rare. The Hundred Years' War in Europe is called precisely that because it is so rare. Even that conflict, which actually lasted 116 years, had many periods of peace in between conflict.

If we use history as our guide, it is likely that most of the time, the Tiwanaku and Wari polities in Moquegua interacted in peace for their mutual self-interests.

The "Masada of the Andes", the great Wari fortification and sacred town of Cerro Baúl in Moquegua.

That is not to say they were not adversaries. As such, they had to maintain defensive postures against each other in case one tried to take advantage of the other. But the historical record is replete with examples of adversaries engaged in simultaneous conflict and trade; conflict and cooperation between states are not mutually exclusive. Eventually, however, the strain of conflict was most certainly a factor in the collapse of both Tiwanaku and Wari by the tenth century AD, and this explains the near simultaneous collapse of Cerro Baúl and the Tiwanaku villages in Moquegua.

Some scholars have argued that the Tiwanaku collapse was due to a drought that destroyed the raised field agricultural systems in the core territory.[65] One scholar has argued that the raised fields formed the underpinnings of the local Tiwanaku economy and that their environmentally-driven collapse was responsible for the cultural decline of the Tiwanaku state.[66] Paleoclimatic research by a number of scholars, plus earlier data from the Quelccaya ice core, indeed supports this idea, given that there is evidence of a drought in the late eleventh century.[67] Quelccaya is a glacier in the central Andes with a precise record of climate changes over many millennia. However, drought in and of itself is insufficient to explain the collapse of Tiwanaku, and there are some problems with the dates of the drought, specifically that in some interpretations of the ice core data, the drought appears a century after the Tiwanaku collapse and not before.

So why did Tiwanaku collapse? The short answer is that we still do not know. The long answer begins with the observation that we know much more than we did a generation ago, and we can eliminate a number of possibilities. First, the collapse of Tiwanaku was slow, and it was not accompanied by a population decline. Archaeological research in the Tiwanaku Valley suggests that roughly the same number of people lived there and in the surrounding areas after AD 1100 as did before the Tiwanaku collapse. Former director of Bolivia's Institute of Archaeology Juan Albarracin-Jordan and Chicago archaeologist James Mathews located almost 1,000 sites in the Tiwanaku Valley after the urban center of Tiwanaku collapsed. This scientific information tells us there was a dispersal of people away from the Tiwanaku capital and not an out-migration of people to other regions in the Andes or a general population decline from disease, lack of food, or some other factor.

The end of Tiwanaku was therefore a political and social organizational phenomenon, not a biological or ecological one, although the drought certainly could have exacerbated an already fragile political situation. Furthermore, the collapse was long and probably occurred over more than three generations (assuming one generation is about 30 years). This political phenomenon was not an immediate crisis, like an invasion of foreigners or a sudden climate change, but was a slower process over several generations. Throughout the southern Titicaca region at least, there are numerous examples of attempts by Tiwanaku peoples to deal effectively with drought conditions by building canals, aqueducts, and reservoirs to feed the fields. By AD 1000, however, the technological limits of these engineering responses had been reached, and other factors kicked in to end Tiwanaku civilization.

The drought of the late eleventh century was indeed a factor in the collapse of Tiwanaku, but it was not the only cause, and appears to have been too late to be the initial factor. In fact, if the Quelccaya ice core data are correct, there was also a drought around AD 650. This is a period after the Tiwanaku peoples had just started their expansion—a time when they would have been a political and economic powerhouse. Of course, one cannot use the drought in the eleventh century to explain collapse, and use the drought in the middle of the seventh century to explain the rise of the state. Had the political and economic organization of Tiwanaku been as strong in the eleventh century as it was in the mid-seventh and eighth centuries, the state would have been able to find alternative means of bringing surplus into the capital to keep the state functioning. The drought helped decentralize an already weak state. It is telling that the Tiwanaku colonial enclave in Moquegua, perhaps the most important one in the west, had fallen out of state orbit before the drought. The same is probably true for the Azapa Valley in northern Chile. In short, there is compelling evidence that the Tiwanaku state was already weakened before the drought set in, as its provincial enclaves were already falling apart. The changing climate on the altiplano was a final straw that broke the state, but it was not the direct or single cause by any means. The destruction of Omo, the Tiwanaku capital

of Moquegua, is another indicator that the weakened state could not withstand the pressures of ecological change and political stress, both internal and external.

We now see that the rise of the post-Tiwanaku kingdoms between AD 1200 and 1400 was partially a result of the drought that peaked around AD 1100 and that the drought was responsible for weakening an already fragile Tiwanaku state. Combined with potential enemies around the lake region, a weakened Tiwanaku military capacity would have left the provincial territories and peripheries inaccessible to Tiwanaku trading caravans. The early collapse of colonial areas such as Moquegua tells us that the loss of exchange routes was a major factor as well in what would have been a complex process of political decline in the Titicaca region. In this sense, the collapse of Tiwanaku was similar to the collapse of other ancient states

Above: The island of Amantaní.
Opposite: Map of the 16th century kingdoms of the Titicaca region.

Azángaro

Callawaya

Chiquicache

Moho

*Señorios of
the Omasuyus*

*Señorío of
the Collas*

•*Hatúncolla*

Paucarcolla

Chucuito

*Island of
the Sun*

Ilave

Juli *Pomata*

Señorío of the Lupacas

*Señorío of
the Pacajes*

50 km

Desaguadero •

throughout history and prehistory—it was relatively slow from the perspective of people experiencing it, and there was no single cause. It was the slow accumulation of factors that led to the collapse of Tiwanaku civilization.

The Great Kingdoms of the Twelfth through Sixteenth Centuries

As Tiwanaku collapsed, a number of smaller independent kingdoms developed in the areas of former Tiwanaku control. In chapter 99 of his famous Crónica, Cieza de León says that the Collao was perhaps the most populous region in Peru. He tells us about the numerous herds of llamas and alpacas and the vast expanses of grasslands in the Titicaca region where they grazed. He describes rich local lords and the poor peasants who worked for them. He tells us that Aymara lords were carried around on litters like the Inca emperor. Cieza describes large towns along the lake edge and tells us about remote territories away from the lake where many people dispersed after the Spanish conquest. He ponders whether the Titicaca region, had it been in a better climate, such as one of the lower valleys where maize could be grown, would have been the best and richest land in all of the Indies.

It is largely from the information in Cieza and other early historians that we learn about the great pre-Inca Aymara señoríos, or kingdoms, of the Titicaca region. In one of his most important quotes about the pre-Inca peoples of the region, Cieza tells us: "Before the Inca reigned, according to many indians from Collao, there was in their province two great lords, one named Zapana and the other Cari, and these lords conquered many pucaras that are their fortifications, and that one of them entered Lake Titicaca, and found on the major island [Isla del Sol] bearded white people with whom they fought and put all of them to death."[68]

Cieza was an astute observer. Along with his work, which provided a great deal of firsthand information from the Inca political class, was that of Bernabé Cobo, Guamán Poma de Ayala, Garcilaso de la Vega, Ramos Gavilán, Juan de Betanzos, and others, who described the peoples and landscapes of the Titicaca area. These kinds of historical documents permit us to define a number of distinct political divisions in the Titicaca region during the sixteenth century that almost certainly reflect some pre-Inca boundaries.

The two largest political groups mentioned in the sixteenth-century texts were the Lupaqa and the Colla. These two kingdoms figure prominently in the oral and written histories of the region as two protagonists engaged in a great military struggle immediately prior to conquest of the region by the Inca. The Lupaqa capital was located at the town of Chucuito in the western lake area. The Lupaqa zone bordered the Colla in the north and extended as far south the Desaguadero bridge. The Lupaqa also apparently controlled the Island of the Sun prior to the Inca conquest. To the south were the Pacajes, located in an area that included the ancestral home of the Tiwanaku state. Other, smaller groups include the Canas, the Canchis to the far north, and the very poorly understood Omasuyus to the east—

also referred to as the Kallawaya. Historian Geoffrey Spurling tells us that Betanzos identified four northern "provinces" of the Titicaca area, including Azángaro, Chiquicache, Moho, and Kallawaya (later Carabaya). If Betanzos is correct, the northeastern and eastern side of the lake would have been divided into a number of divisions, smaller than those on the western side, reflecting the traditionally fractured political organization of that area throughout history and prehistory.[69] This map shows these ethnic and political regions in the Andes prior to the Spanish conquest.[70] These boundaries existed well before the Spanish conquest and were based upon Inca provincial boundaries, according to historian Catherine Julien.[71]

In other words, the collapse of Tiwanaku led to a familiar situation in world history: the breakdown of a large state or empire and the emergence of culturally similar but competing smaller political groups. Sometimes referred to as balkanization, this situation inevitably begins with a period of great instability as different groups vie for power while the military capacity of the earlier state wanes. Conflict is virtually inevitable, as we see throughout the southern Andes after Tiwanaku collapsed. In the greater Titicaca region, more than a dozen large and scores of small political groups rose in the twelfth through fifteenth centuries before Inca armies swept down and united them into a single province of their immense empire.

Many historical documents tell us much about the Titicaca political landscape in this period after he Tiwanaku collapse. The largest cultural and geographical divisions in Titicaca-area society were Umasuyu and Urqusuyu. Umasuyu corresponds geographically to the eastern and northeastern side of the lake, while Urqusuyu refers to the western and northwestern side. These concepts, however, are more than just geographical terms. They refer to a series of dualities vital to Andean political and social geography. *Urqu*, or *orqo*, implies masculinity, "mountainness," dryness, solidity, and height.[72] In Bertonio's dictionary, *orqo* is defined as "the masculine sex in all of the brute animals." In contrast, *uma* refers to femininity, water, wetness, passivity, and lowness.[73] The boundary between these two concepts was the lake itself, expressed in the term *taypi*, roughly translated as "middle."[74] Some political

A prehistoric bridge in the Pajchiri area of Bolivia.

divisions were geographically associated conceptually divided between Umasuyu and Urqusuyu. The division follows more or less the middle of the lake, the Desaguadero River, and Lake Poopó. For example, the Canas was divided into Canas Urqusuyu and Canas Umasuyu. Likewise, Pacajes was divided into Pacajes Urqusuyu and Pacajes Umasuyu, and so on.

The dictionary compiled by Ludovico Bertonio provides information on political offices in Aymara society during the sixteenth century. He provides a rich and varied vocabulary of post-Tiwanaku Aymara society. He lists a number of terms in use in the early colonial period (circa 1532 to 1700) that indicate a rich vocabulary on political and social rank. One implication of this vocabulary is that the Lupaqa and Colla were kingdoms of some complexity. This idea is reinforced by several quotes by Cieza: "The principal señores are always well attended and when they are on the road they are carried on litters."[75] Being carried in litters was considered one of the marks of kingship or very high social and political status in Andean society. In this light, Lupaqa social and political structure was characterized by a typically Andean dual social and political organization, with the two divisions known as Hanansaya and Urinsaya, respectively.

This dual organization characterized all seven of the main Lupaqa settlements except Juli, where the lower Urinsaya was further subdivided in two. Lupaqa leaders were addressed by the hereditary title *cari*, a term more or less meaning "king." The population of the Lupaqa area was immense, and Lupaqa elite had retainers known as *yana*, a title indicating an inferior social status of a group attached in a vassal-like relationship to royalty. The Lupaqa elite were very rich in material resources and had enormous social prestige and political power. Lupaqa elite are said to have owned thousands of camelids, while their yana and the tax-paying peasantry got by with a subsistence-level way of life. In short, prior to conquest of the region by the Inca, the Collao was populated by a number of political groups of varying size, with the Lupaqa and the Colla being the largest.

It appears that the great Aymara kingdoms were able to come together in times of need, particularly when facing threats from their neighbors, and create elaborate forts and fearsome armies of impressive proportions. In the absence of such threats, however, the Aymara jealously guarded their freedom to move their herds and live in villages across the landscape. It is most likely that the concept of the Choquela that we mentioned earlier—a person who lives outside the authority of a king or sovereign—had its origins in twelfth- to fifteenth-century Aymara life or, at the very earliest, in the preceding Tiwanaku period in the seventh through eleventh centuries. It is no surprise that in the short time the Incas held control over the Titicaca region, there were at least four very bloody rebellions by Aymara inhabitants that had to be viciously repressed by the Cusco authorities.

The Colla were another large and powerful political group in the Titicaca area during the immediate pre-Inca periods. The Colla were located somewhere slightly south of the Puno area, bounded by the Canas and Canchis areas in the north, probably at the pass of La Raya. The capital of the Colla polity is often said to be the town of Hatuncolla, although it appears that the actual pre-Inca site was the settlement behind the modern town. The great chulpa cemetery site and pilgrimage destination of Sillustani was in Colla territory as well and was almost certainly one of the great religious centers of the pre-Inca Titicaca world. It is very probable that if the Inca had not emerged from their homeland in the central Andes when they did, either the Colla or the Lupaqa would have conquered the Andes to become as powerful as the Inca. In fact, several early historians, most notably Montesinos, call the Colla an empire, with influence throughout the area of former Tiwanaku control. While most archaeologists today do not see the Colla as so powerful, the fact that an early writer mentions this suggests that they had an influence far beyond that of a simple tribal society.

The Pacajes area was the ancestral home of the Tiwanaku state. The peoples of the Pacajes after the Tiwanaku collapse established their towns and villages in

A chulpa in the Ilave region.

the Tiwanaku Valley and immediate surroundings. To the east of the lake were the mysterious Omasuyus and Larecaja regions. These areas are very poorly known, but even the little archaeological work that has been done indicates the existence of very rich societies after Tiwanaku throughout the region.

The great chronicler Guamán Poma de Ayala describes the pre-Inca periods throughout the central Andes as "*auca runa,*" or the age of warriors and a time of strife. This description undoubtedly reflected "official" histories of the Inca Empire that often sought to denigrate the earlier cultures the Inca had conquered. On the other hand, scholars since Cobo have recognized that *pukaras*, or hill forts, throughout the Andes most likely were built during this period, although the construction of massive fortified sites began as early as the first millennium BC on the coast. While

A chulpa in the north near Arapa.

the construction of hill forts has a long tradition in the central Andes, the number of such forts dramatically increased in the post-Tiwanaku period. This indicates a relatively high level of conflict during this period. The immediate pre-Inca period in the Titicaca area is no exception, and, as discussed earlier, such a political landscape replete with conflict is the norm in human history after the collapse of a large empire.

Pukaras can be seen just about everywhere in the Titicaca region. Some of the largest are truly enormous, such as the massive ones at Pukara Juli and Tanka Tanka. These huge *pukaras* have massive walls encircling a very large area, with houses near the base and alongside the lowest defensive wall. These are the classic fortified hilltop sites found throughout the altiplano and originally described by Bernabé Cobo in the early histories. These sites almost always are surrounded by at

Following pages: The site of Cutimbo in the high altiplano above Puno.

least three large defensive walls, and some have as many as six. These walls reach as high as three meters, and some are as wide as two meters. The width of the walls is significant because it indicates a tactic in which defenders would run along the top of the wall, not just use it as a shield. The walled areas of the major pukaras were big enough to enclose agricultural areas, pasture areas, and springs. This appears to be the strategy for these late pukaras: provide defense for not only the people inside but for agricultural lands and grazing areas. This strategy would have allowed people to withstand a siege for a long time, since they had water from springs, and plants and animals all within the fortress. The early historian Montesinos described an Inca fortress in the north Titicaca region: "[T]he whole stronghold formed a cone, and the entire army was within the andenes [defensive walls]." He further described the pukara as built with many "andenes, trenches and so on in such a way that they each had but one very narrow entrance. . . all the way up [the hill] . . . where the king had his stores and the necessary supplies."[76] Fortresses were central to the life of the peoples of the Titicaca region during this time. In many ways, they are as impressive as monuments as the more sublime pyramids and palaces of Tiwanaku.

One of the most famous features of the later prehistoric periods of the Titicaca region is the development of burial towers. In his dictionary, Bertonio lists *uta amaya*, an Aymara term for "house of the soul." This is probably the technically correct name for these aboveground burials, but they have been called for more than a century "chulpas". Chulpas are made of stone or adobe; they are towers that were the final repositories for the dead. Chulpa architecture varies throughout the central Andes. Classic examples are found at the site of Sillustani in the northwestern Titicaca region. These towers are square or round and reach several meters in height. Some are constructed out of finely carved Inca-style masonry, particularly those at Sillustani. Most other chulpas are more modest in construction and are built out of fieldstones or adobe. Larger chulpas are also constructed out of adobe, well-fitted fieldstones, poorly fitted fieldstones, and cut blocks.

The chulpa phenomenon represents a radical change in the treatment of the dead after the collapse of Tiwanaku around the twelfth century. For the first time,

The interior chamber of a very large chulpa in Cutimbo. Note the niches in the wall.

tombs were visible on the surface. The earliest dated aboveground tomb architecture comes from a site in the upper Moquegua region. In this valley, known as Otora, research discovered a typical belowground tomb of the Tiwanaku period—a hole about 40 centimeters wide and 50 centimeters deep with a single body—with a circular wall above. Offerings were found inside the circular wall; the offerings date to the late twelfth/early thirteenth century. This earliest "collar tomb" represents the first use of ground space to mark a burial.

The big difference between above- and below ground tombs is obviously visibility. A burial in the ground, often in a cemetery or under a house floor, did not leave any ritual area that could be found with any ease. There is no evidence of tombstones or other kinds of markers on the graves prior to the chulpas. In

Following pages: Chulpas from the site of Sillustani.
Photo on the bottom of page 142 courtesy of E. Klarich.

other words, the new cultural innovation of the post-Tiwanaku period includes the marking of burial spaces of ancestors. These spaces were made sacred, and people repeatedly visited these graves and left various kinds of offerings. In the tomb in Otora mentioned above, the offerings included pottery, guinea pigs, cloth, maize, and other plants.

The second big difference in the chulpa burial practice is that people started putting many more individuals in the tombs. Tiwanaku and earlier tombs had only one or at most two individuals. When there were two bodies, the tomb almost always contained a female adult and child. These tombs were below the ground, out of sight, and apparently not revisited in any meaningful ways. Chulpas, on the other hand, were not intended for individuals but for groups. Most chulpas contain the remains of numerous individuals, suggesting that they were more like mausoleums than simple burials. Whole groups, most likely families, were interred in the chulpas. Some anthropologists have argued that the development of chulpas represents the first kin-based identities that we understand as ayllu in the Andes, while others have argued that the collapse of the earlier states gave rise to more village-oriented social practices that focused on the small-kin group and some kind of larger religion or other belief. Whatever the case, the rise of the chulpa burial practices represents one of the great changes in the Andes in the twelfth century.

The traveler to the Titicaca region is able to visit many fortresses with chulpa burials. The large fortress outside the town of Juli, near kilometer 76 on the Puno–Desaguadero highway in the western lake region, is one of the largest in the Titicaca region. As one approaches Juli from the north, Pukara Juli is the huge mountain to the west that rises above the town on the opposite side of the highway. It ranks as one of the largest pukaras in the entire Andes. Pukara Juli was one of the first archaeological monuments to be described by the Spanish historians. Bernabé Cobo tells us about the conquest of the Titicaca region by the famous emperor Pachacuti Inca and refers to this fortress, where the inhabitants of the Juli region took refuge:

On this expedition the Inca subjugated all the towns and nations surrounding

the great Lake Titicaca . . . which were densely populated at that time. Some of the towns defended themselves bravely, and they had many clashes with the Inca before they were subjugated. The Inca subjected many of them to a relentless siege, and they built forts in order to defend themselves, such as . . . the one we see on the high hill near the town of Juli, which has five dry stone walls, one inside the other, where the natives took refuge and fought for a long time in defending themselves.[77]

The settlement of Pukara Juli was actually a series of hamlets and villages that surrounded the fortification walls. This is in fact the classic pattern for these major forts. The walls on Pukara Juli are truly massive. We calculate that the principal defensive walls were approximately two meters high and about two meters wide in antiquity. The construction was a double-wall, rubble-fill technique, making the walls very strong and wide enough for defenders to walk on. There were, as accurately described by Cobo, five walls progressively placed up the hill.

On the slope up the north side of Pukara Juli is a section of wall that provides some additional insight into the nature of the defensive strategies of the inhabitants. At one of the least naturally defensible areas, there is a wide cleared area in front of the slope leading up to a major wall. The rubble from this area was placed in front of the wall to make the ascent exceedingly difficult, a technique well known in ancient forts from around the world.[78] Even today, walking on the rubble is extremely difficult. Not surprisingly, the area of the rubble contained a high density of throwing stones, evidence of actual conflict at the site of Pukara Juli. Indeed, it is a brilliant strategy. Imagine as you stare at Pukara Juli from the road the hundreds of people massed behind these huge walls as they withstood sieges. They had their llamas and alpacas, springs, potato fields, and plenty of stored water in huge ceramic vessels lined up and ready for any siege. If the besiegers left even for a few days, the villagers could return to their plots down below. It would have been a formidable defense, one that would eventually require the full muscle of the Inca to overcome.

Excavations at the Yacari–Tuntachawi area of Pukara Juli by archaeologist Edmundo de la Vega from the National Technical University of the Altiplano–Puno discovered a large number of storage vessels on the site. De la Vega discovered double-chambered, undecorated vessels buried on small terraces (One of these can be seen in the museum in Pucara). De la Vega analyzed a number of very small structures (less than 1.5 meters in diameter) that he concluded were for storage as well. In other words, the excavation evidence indicates a site designed to store food and possibly water and to protect crops and animals. All these features were ultimately created to protect the population against a sustained siege—a population that lived at the base of the pukara and in the surrounding villages and hamlets.

Another major pukara of the Lupaqa area is known as Cutimbo. The site is located a little more than 22 kilometers south of Puno on a mesa more than 4,000 meters above sea level.[79] According to the late archaeologist John Hyslop, the site is at least 25 hectares in size. He also describes the many round house foundations found on the site, representing a large prehistoric residential area spread over the entire mesa. Cutimbo has many beautiful chulpas, some of the most beautiful in the Andes. Many of the chulpas were built with Inca stone masonry techniques. The chulpas at Cutimbo, like many others in the region, had an occasional bas-relief carving. Cutimbo was most likely the residence and burial grounds of the Lupaqa elite prior to Inca expansion. Archaeologist Rolando Paredes tells us that the largest chulpa at Cutimbo was used as an ushnu, or Inca temple platform, as well as a burial tower. He discovered some incredibly beautiful large Inca pottery vessels that can be seen in a very nice exhibit at the museum below the site. Cutimbo also has a series of rock art panels along the lower side of the site, facing the museum. This art is late in prehistory and possibly even colonial in date and is most likely contemporary with the Inca or early Spanish site.

The Pilgrimage Destination of Sillustani

As the Colla emerged as the largest kingdom in the region, the people converted an older site into a great regional pilgrimage destination at the village of Sillustani. This village was part of the Hatuncolla complex during the Inca period. Sillustani is one of the most famous places in highland Peru or Bolivia. It is located squarely in Colla territory, due west of the plains between Juliaca and Paucarcolla near beautiful Lake Umayo. It is also near the sixteenth-century boundary between Aymara and Quechua speakers and is most likely near the late prehistoric border between the Lupaqa and the Colla. This border is marked by a number of large pukaras. University of Pittsburgh archaeologist Elizabeth Arkush tells us that the great fortresses were mostly built in the fourteenth and fifteenth centuries AD. The date of the construction of these fortresses indicates a strategic focus on the emerging Inca Empire to the north. The builders may also have had some concerns with people from the south in what was the Pacajes area where Tiwanaku was located.

Sillustani housed a number of spectacular Inca period chulpa burial towers that became the focus of pilgrims from all groups in the region, including the Lupaqa to the south, the traditional enemy of the Colla.[80] This pilgrimage site was clearly linked politically, economically, and ritually to the huge town of Hatuncolla a few kilometers away. Hatuncolla, as described below, was the main town and garrison of the Inca in the region. Sillustani has chulpas of virtually all the different types found throughout the greater Titicaca region. There is no other site quite like this in terms of chulpa variability. In virtually all areas of the Titicaca region and beyond, there are usually only one or two types of chulpas on any particular site. Not at Sillustani. We find virtually every kind of chulpa. There are, for instance, very poorly constructed ones built in the so-called igloo style, adobe chulpas, round chulpas, square ones, and at least one built in what would appear to be a derived Tiwanaku style. Some of the larger chulpas are clearly Inca in date, though they may have been rewalled in Inca times using fine masonry techniques.

The great fortress or pucara known as Pucara Juli from the period of the Great Kingdoms.

The most likely explanation is that Sillustani was a great pan-Aymara pilgrimage destination, where prominent people from a huge region came and buried their dead in the style of their homes. Given the importance of pilgrimages in Andean society, it is likely that Sillustani was the center of rituals for all the different peoples of the region, something akin to Delphi for the ancient Greeks. Looking at the chulpas, one can imagine the adobe ones painted in bright colors, particularly yellow, white, and red. Perhaps cloth or even gold was attached to large chulpas for special events, where peoples from all over the region would come to celebrate, pray, gossip, trade, and feast.

Sillustani was not just a cemetery and pilgrimage destination. There was a large residential area on the west side of the site. Approximately three hectares of village land was located on the hills flanking the modern entrance to the site, under and adjacent to the present-day road.[81] We can surmise that after Tiwanaku collapsed, the people in this village claimed the status as caretakers of the Sillustani pilgrimage shrine, replacing the great Tiwanaku-period centers at Esteves Island

near Puno and more importantly the Island of the Sun. Certainly, the existence of pilgrimage destinations is well documented for the prehispanic Andes in general and the Titicaca region in particular. An example is the Island of the Sun, where the Inca maintained the pilgrimage destination during their occupation. The center at Sillustani was one such highly charged sacred place, built prior to the arrival of the Inca Empire in the region.[82]

That the collapse of the first pan-Titicaca pilgrimage shrine, built on the Island of the Sun during the Tiwanaku period, is coincident with the collapse of Tiwanaku is quite telling and suggests a certain type of political and ritual dynamic in the region. In other words, the Tiwanaku state constructed the first pan-Aymara huaca and pilgrimage destination on the Island of the Sun. The collapse of this massive island-wide huaca correlated with the collapse of the Tiwanaku political structure and the emergence of Sillustani as a regional pilgrimage and political center. This shift would correlate to the decline of the Pacajes (ancestral Tiwanaku) region as the principal political power and a shift to the north in Colla territory. The control of the one panregional pilgrimage destination during and after Tiwanaku therefore correlated with the center of political power. The numerous precious objects recovered by Lima archaeologist Ruiz Estrada at Sillustani are virtually unique for the greater Titicaca region. His work supports the idea that Sillustani was a pilgrimage destination, because this is exactly the pattern that we see for the Tiwanaku and Inca periods on the Island of the Sun.[83] As described below, people from many areas came to the Island of the Sun on pilgrimages and left valuable offerings. The Colla to the north developed as the most powerful polity in the post-Tiwanaku periods, and they correspondingly created and co-opted the most sacred place in the Titicaca area.

The Inca Conquest of the Titicaca Region

The Quechua-speaking peoples who lived in the Cusco region built a mighty conquest state that expanded over an enormous area in a relatively short span of time. In less than 150 years, the Inca conquered a region more than 3,500 kilometers long and

Opposite: An early Inca pottery vessel found near the town of Huatasani.

covering 1,000,000 square kilometers. Over the centuries, scholars have defined and redefined the nature of the Inca Empire, with descriptions ranging from a totalitarian state to a benevolent "socialist" empire. In the nineteenth century, North American and British writers sought to portray the Spaniards in as negative a light as possible and simultaneously emphasized the positive qualities of the peoples the Spanish conquered, including the Inca. In a similar vein, twentieth-century writers interpreted the Inca more as a great redistributive state, in which even the poorest citizens were protected from disease and want.

Such romantic illusions aside, the historical and archaeological information clearly shows us that the Inca Empire was a classic conquest state with a professional army corps and massive bureaucracy. As with virtually every other imperial state in history, the motive for Inca expansion was territorial gain, the acquisition of resources, and the neutralization of potential enemies. The idea that the Inca Empire was a benign state concerned with commoners' welfare simply fails the test of scholarship. The vaunted road and storehouse system, for instance, was used largely

for strategic military purposes and was not some kind of social welfare program to help the poor. Fundamental requirements for ancient empires were the efficient and rapid movement of the army to suppress rebellion, and the movement of provisions for the army. The Incas were masters of military engineering, and their great road system must be seen in that light.

The leaders of the Inca Empire used traditional Andean principles to build their state. The conquest of new territories was often preceded by intense negotiations and political intrigue. After a territory was conquered, the Inca usually instituted their classic incorporation strategies, including the rehabilitation of the existing road system, the building of tambos, or way stations, the resettling of colonists, and the co-option of local political authority. Physical facilities were constructed by using a labor tax, based usually on the decimal system of labor organization.[84] In this system, taxpayers were divided into a series of levels, such as 10,000, 5,000, 1,000, 500, 100, 50, and 10. Each level had a supervisor, who allocated laborers depending upon the task at hand. Conquered territories were ideally divided into three political categories: state lands, church lands, and land that remained in the hands of local peoples. The Inca made sure that the indigenous elite were left intact and incorporated into the imperial hierarchy, as long as they did not have a history of rebellion against the state.

The Titicaca area was one of the most important, if not the most important, provinces in the Inca Empire. Evidence of the Inca Empire is everywhere. The archaeologist Elizabeth Arkush documented numerous cut stones throughout the region, like the one found outside of Juli on the road from Puno. Known as the Inca's Chair and named by the great explorer Ephraim Squier in the nineteenth century, this carving is associated with rituals involving liquids. The stone is similar to the many kenkos and other cut-stone features in the Cusco region.

Near the Inca's Chair, and almost certainly associated with this cut-stone outcrop, is the famous carving Altarani. We learned about this carving briefly in the legends section of this book; New Agers describe it as a doorway to somewhere very special not of this world. Scholars have a more prosaic but equally fascinating

Opposite: The town of Ollantaytambo in the Sacred Valley in the Cusco region. The layout of this town is similar to many Inca cities in the Titicaca region.

interpretation of Altarani. This huge carving in a rock outcrop is made in classic Titicaca regional style, reminiscent of iconography on the Island of the Moon and at the Inca Uyu in Chucuito. Perhaps the most fascinating aspect of the Altarani carving is that it is not finished. As can be seen in the photograph, the left side has a squared-off section. To the right, one can still see the marks where the stonemasons were working at the time they stopped. Given its association with Inca carved stones in the region, plus other evidence, scholars see the carving of Altarani as an example of a common ritual practice among the Inca. The fact that the style of carving is a fusion of Inca and local Titicaca regional canons, and that it was in the semi-allied territory of the Lupaqas, strongly suggests that this was a locally inspired ritual area conducted with the Inca Empire's knowledge and consent, if not outright direction. It is likely that this was one of many carved rocks along the Urqusuyu road that formed a pilgrimage path for people during the Inca occupation.

The Inca province of Collasuyu had an enormous population and was economically very rich. Some of the most important resources of the prehispanic Andes, including potatoes, quinoa, fish, llamas, direct access to gold in the forests, and even maize obtained from certain areas of the altiplano, were found in the Titicaca region. Within a one- or two-day walk from the lake were regions that had timber, coca, cotton, maize, animal pelts, silver, hallucinogenic substances, and other valued commodities. There are thousands of Inca sites throughout the greater Titicaca region. Inca control and influence extended well beyond the borders of the Titicaca area, south to the Atacama Desert in central Chile. Inca sites, in fact, are ubiquitous throughout desert areas of the Pacific coast.

There are literally tens of thousands of archaeological sites in the greater Titicaca region that date to the Inca period. This was a time of huge population increases and great political changes in the entire Andes, from southern Ecuador to central Chile. The Incas moved people from defensible hilltop locations down into the valley bottoms and into the vast plains. They concentrated local people into small cities and towns, moved villages and hamlets closer to roads, built religious shrines, and organized communal labor throughout their realm. In the Titicaca region, Inca

A Google Earth image of Hatuncolla, the capital of the Colla Kingdom and Inca center
The site of Sillustani is just up the road to the northwest a few kilometers.

administrators created about a dozen urban sites. These cities were known by the Spanish word cabecera, which meant the most important political and economic center of a region. Our research shows that virtually all the cabeceras on the Peruvian side of Lake Titicaca—Hatuncolla, Puno, Ilave, Chucuito, Acora, Zepita, Juli, Yunguyu, and others—were founded by the Inca state. They were created by the forced movement of people from the hills and valleys into these new urban centers. A few cabeceras stand out as particularly interesting.

The largest cabecera in the greater Titicaca region is Hatuncolla (The name means "Great Collao"). It was one of four regional administrative centers in the Inca Empire, according to Spanish historian Cieza de León, along with Hatun Xauxa, Pumpu, and Huánuco Pampa. In the late 16th century, Cieza wrote:

Following pages: 154-155 An Inca wall at the site of Raqchi, near Sicuani; 156-157 the carved rock at the site of Altarani, near Juli.

Hatuncolla in past times was the grandest thing in the Collao, and locals affirm that before the Incas subjected them, they were under the authority of Zapana and his descendents … and afterward the Inca adorned this town with buildings and many storehouses where by their command the tribute that was brought from the fields were stored, and they had a temple of the Sun with many mamaconas and priests to serve the temple, and a number of mitimaes [colonists] and warriors placed in the frontier.[85]

In other words, Hatuncolla site was a major center, complete with a state temple, storehouses, and residences for Inca administrators. Hatuncolla is the largest of the Inca sites of the Collao. It is built on a slightly modified grid pattern that archaeologists refer to as orthogonal. The orthogonal pattern has slightly angled streets radiating out of one or two principal plazas. The difference between a Spanish and an Inca one is the intentional angling of the streets out of the main plaza.

In Hatuncolla, as at other cabeceras, we find many cut-stone blocks in Inca style. Cut-stone blocks are costly to create, of course, and the fact that they are still found in many buildings in these centers shows us how impressive the old cities would have been to the visitor and resident alike. The modern village of Hatuncolla is approximately 30 hectares in size. The Inca-period size of Hatuncolla was two to three times that. According to early historian Cieza de León, Emperor Pachacuti used Hatuncolla as a garrison to quarter soldiers to maintain a military presence in the region. This historical evidence clearly tells us that Hatuncolla was the center of Inca military and political efforts to control the Collao.[86]

In the Visita of Viceroy Francisco Toledo of the late sixteenth century, Hatuncolla is listed as having a total population of about 2,300, including people described as "aymaraes," "urus," and "hatunlunas." We learn from this incredible historical document what the people here had to provide in tribute to the Inca authorities: silver, animals, chuño, cloth, and fish. This great town, that just 40 years earlier had had thousands of administrators, soldiers, retainers, and workers, was reduced to a mere 2,000 and some souls after the Inca collapse. For whatever reason, Hatuncolla declined after the collapse of the Inca Empire. One could conjecture that Hatuncolla was populated by immigrant Inca officials during the occupation and that the collapse of the empire at the hands of Francisco Pizarro led to an abandonment of the center. At any rate, by the late sixteenth century, Hatuncolla was a minor town in the Titicaca region, a spectacular decline from its power during Inca imperial times.

Hatuncolla was the main Inca center for the northern Titicaca region and for the province as a whole. The second most important town in the province, and the largest of the Inca centers in the western and southwestern Lupaqa region, was Chucuito. Chucuito is located approximately 16 kilometers south of Puno on the Puno–Desaguadero highway. It was located directly adjacent to the Inca highway. The site was the home of Martín Cari and Martín Cusi, the two principal caciques, or local lords, of Lupaqa in 1564. Chucuito was therefore the capital of the Lupaqa kingdom. Historical documents tell us that laborers were sent from the six other Lupaqa towns to Chucuito for service in the households of these caciques, a fact that highlights the importance of this town during this period.

We have already discussed one of the most enigmatic buildings in the Titicaca region, the Inca temple known as the Inca Uyu, that is found at the site of Chucuito. The Inca Uyu was built in an Inca provincial style with massive cut-stone blocks. It was found in what was the earlier Inca plaza area. We have seen how the New Age tour industry has turned this building into a fertility temple, changing the original word uyu, meaning "corral" or "cemetery," into uyo, supposedly "penis" in Quechua. The site is now a major destination for New Age tourism due in no small part to the phallic carvings found inside the building. A number of nonphallic pieces have been collected from the surrounding countryside. These were most likely stones that projected out of sacred Inca agricultural terracing or other buildings, as can be seen at scores of other sites in the highlands, such as Pisac. The rest of the more unusual pieces are almost certainly recent productions, made probably in the last thirty years and assembled by local authorities and private individuals interested in promoting the tourist trade. Chucuito is a fun site, well worth the visit for both the interesting archaeology and the fantastic stories.

The pioneering archaeologist Marion Tschopik first excavated at the building. Her research showed that the Inca Uyu was in fact Inca in date. According to the late great archaeologist John Hyslop, all the levels she excavated had some Spanish colonial glazed wares or glass, and she therefore was not certain of its context. Because of this, the excavation results have never been fully published. According to Hyslop, Tschopik learned of a structure called Kurinuyu, located east of Inca Uyu, that had existed in living memory up to the 1940s. This second temple is not surprising, as it fits in well with Inca concepts of duality as it was practiced in the Titicaca area. The Kurinuyu was most likely located in what is now the modern plaza. The beautiful church in the plaza was most likely built over the Inca ushnu, or elevated temple structure.

The cut stone at Inca Uyu is not in a typical Cusco style. It represents a poorly known architectural technique within Inca stylistic canons.[87] Several blocks have an elongated U shape that has counterparts in Inca sites such as Machu Picchu, Raqchi, and Ollantaytambo. At the latter sites, the blocks formed the bottom part of niches and windows. We can therefore presume that typical Inca niches and windows characterized this building.[88]

Hyslop says that Chucuito had two plazas, one at the location of the modern plaza and the second near the Inca Uyu. Indeed, standing next to the Inca Uyu, one can imagine a large Inca plaza that would have existed in the early sixteenth century. Chucuito is comparable only to Hatuncolla in size and importance in the Inca period in the Titicaca region. There is little doubt that it was the principal site in the Lupaqa area and a major administrative center for the Inca Empire in the Titicaca area.

Another major ancient town along the Inca road is called Paucarcolla. It is located just above the plains that cover the landscape northwest of the lake. These plains are famous in the early Inca-period history of the region. The historical documents tell us that the Lupaqa and Colla were fighting each other for regional control. Other documents suggest that both were fighting the Canas and Canchis, who lived over the La Raya Pass to the northwest. At this point, with so much interethnic strife in the Titicaca area, the Inca started their aggressive move to the south, taking advantage of the political turmoil. The Inca moved south and conquered the Canas and Canchis and established their city at Raqchi. With this victory, the Inca began a series of political maneuvers against the people of the Collao.

Inca armies almost certainly massed at Raqchi again, ready to cross the pass at La Raya and attack the Aymara heartland. The first move of the Incas was against the town of Ayaviri in an Aymara-speaking region. The town resisted, and there was a great slaughter of the inhabitants. The Inca then planned their move to the lake region. Spies were everywhere. Colla leaders secretly met with the Inca emissaries, but so did the Lupaqa.[89] Fearing an Inca–Lupaqa alliance, the Colla initiated an attack against the Lupaqa. Historian Cieza de León says that in the plains above Paucarcolla, 150,000 troops came together for a great battle between the two powerful Aymara kingdoms. Cieza says that at this battle, 30,000 warriors died, including the Colla king. The battle ended with a decisive victory for the Lupaqa. The Inca were very disappointed in being unable to take advantage of the conflict, and the battle permitted the Lupaqa to become the principal political power in the Titicaca region for a brief time.[90] The town of Paucarcolla was at the center of this battle, being near the border between the Lupaqa and the Inca. Paucarcolla was the third largest Inca town in the Titicaca region, smaller than only Chucuito and Hatuncolla.[91]

In the early colonial period, Paucarcolla was a modest-sized town, but during Inca times it was a large town of at least 25 hectares. The site had more than 4,500 residents, making it almost twice the size of the former Inca regional capital at Hatuncolla.[92] Paucarcolla was divided into Aymaras and Urus, with the latter making up nine percent of the total population. It is interesting to note In the Tasa of Toledo that apart from the usual tribute items such as meat and wool, the people of Paucarcolla also contributed dried fish and salt. The area therefore was most likely important for salt production in the Inca period as well, although we have no direct archaeological evidence of this at the present time. Unlike Hatuncolla, Paucarcolla was on the main Inca highway from Cusco to the south. It also had a large pre-Inca population on the hill to the east of the modern highway, known as Santa Barbara

Paucarcolla.

Farther along the lake to the south is a beautiful little town called Juli. Juli is sometimes called Little Rome of the Altiplano, due to the magnificent churches that can still be seen in the town. In fact, Juli was the political center of early colonial life in the Titicaca region. The Spaniards felt that Juli was a better location than either Hatuncolla or Chucuito for several reasons. First, it was in the center of the western road, roughly midway between the northern and southern shores of the lake. The western road out of Juli went directly to the very important valley of Moquegua. Moquegua was a major wine-producing area in southern Peru. In addition, the density of Inca and early colonial indigenous populations in Juli was surprisingly high, belying colonial documents that stressed the importance of Hatuncolla and Chucuito in the immediate contact period.

Early ecclesiastical officials flocked to Juli and set up its many churches. It is therefore not surprising that Juli boasted the first printing press in the highlands and was a center of Jesuit and later Dominican orders. According to the early censuses,

Cusillo dancers in Juli in 1988.

Juli was the largest early colonial town, as determined by the total number of tax-paying males in 1567. Archaeological evidence indicates that it was a major Inca-period settlement, reaching about 20 hectares in size. Excavations in and near Juli indicate a substantial Inca use of the town. There is very fancy Inca pottery, both imported and locally made. It was most likely a major pottery-making center and possibly a brewing factory as well. A little outside of town, on the San Bartolomé hill, is a town called Olla, possibly a reference to an earlier pottery-making center.

Juli is on the Inca road, and, in fact, a branch of the road went around the hill of Sapacolla, or "Sleeping Lion," behind Juli. This fact tells us that Juli was the principal settlement in the western Titicaca region, because the main road forked at its entrance and reconnected in the center of Juli. This well-paved road leads out of

A section of the Inca road above the town of Moho on the eastern or Omasuyu side of the Lake.

the town south toward Pomata. Juli is also built on an orthogonal grid pattern typical of important Inca administrative centers.

Juli is home to a fascinating annual festival with a tinku-type contest with people dressed as cusillos. Tinku is a kind of ritual battle that is traditional to the Andes. It usually involves entire communities over several days. Most often the ritual battles are not violent, but on occasion some people are hurt and in very instances people are even accidently killed. The tinku in Juli represents the great epic battles between the Inca and the local peoples. This ritual battle lasts for days with hundreds of people participating or watching the ceremonies. Ultimately, the Inca win by sheer force, but the "battle" is noble and controlled eventually ending up at the base of the cathedral. In 1988 I witnessed a complete cusillo event. The "battle" raged for days, with much good drink and cheer in between. Virtually the entire town was there and merchants plied their wares as well. These kinds of events are found throughout the Peruvian and Bolivian altiplano.

Inca Roads in the Lake Region

The Inca Empire was famous for its vast network of roads throughout the Andes. Apart from economic and military functions, the road system had administrative and even ideological functions within the Inca Empire as well.[93] Much of the road system across the empire was not built by the Inca themselves but was co-opted from earlier roads. The University of California, Santa Barbara archaeologist Katharina Schreiber and other scholars have demonstrated that the "Inca" road system in the Carahuarazo Valley in the central highlands was actually built earlier by the Wari state.[94] Our research in the Titicaca region confirms this, with large numbers of pre-Inca sites located adjacent to the ancient road. The Inca inherited the trade routes and roads of earlier cultures and used their enormous labor capacity to staff and improve this communication system. The vast system of tambos, or way stations, and the construction of excellent bridges are two examples of this road-maintenance policy. The famous "floating" totora bridge across the Río Desaguadero is an example of an Inca construction that lasted into the nineteenth century.[95] Cieza de León described this bridge as being made of "sheaves of oats" that were strong enough to hold horses and men. These sheaves were most likely totora reeds that grow in the lake. He also said there were toll collectors at the bridge in the time of the Inca. Alongside the bridges were causeways built over swampy land. Today, the remains of such constructions can be seen outside Chucuito, near Sillustani, and near Pajchiri in the south. The effect of this policy was to give the Inca an enormous strategic advantage against rebellious populations and the ability to move goods over long distances for relatively low costs.

    As one of the most important provinces in the Inca Empire, the Titicaca region had two major roads running roughly northwest–southeast along both sides of the lake. The terms Urqusuyu and Umasuyu referred to the large spatial division of Collasuyu and were also the names of the two branches of the road system in the Titicaca region.[96] John Hyslop conducted the only systematic study of the Inca road system in the Titicaca region, and the following observations are excerpted from his excellent 1984 book.[97] He found that the Titicaca roads were three to seven meters wide. He also found little evidence of margin markers, prepared roadbeds, or sidewalls, although these latter features occasionally occurred in special areas such as the Island of the Sun. The causeway in Lake Umayo, near Sillustani, is part of the Inca road system. The road is visible slightly to the south in Hatuncolla and can be picked up five kilometers northwest of Paucarcolla as well. The road entered Puno and went south between the hills and the lake. Puno was a large Inca town as well. The Inca road enters Chucuito and passes into the plaza, going right past the Inca Uyu, discussed above. South of Chucuito the road becomes a causeway to cross over the swampy zone between the Chucuito hills and the lake edge. My own observations suggest that the Inca reused an old aqueduct as a bed for this causeway. According to

A rehabilitated Inca road on the Island of the Sun.

Hyslop, the Inca road then goes through all the main towns of the lakeside, including Acora, Ilave, Juli, Pomata, and Zepita. Each of these towns also had major early colonial settlements. The town of Zepita is smaller today than in the past, but the spectacular colonial church attests to its importance in the early colonial period.

The Inca roads are famous for the efficient messenger system of the chasquis. Chasquis were runners who manned posts along the highway system and rapidly carried messages or small goods to all parts of the empire. Bernabé Cobo specifically mentions small chasqui stations located along the Collao royal highways:

Apart from the tambos and storehouses, along these two royal highways every quarter of a league there were also some huts or small houses built in pairs facing one another near the road, and these huts were only large enough for two men to fit in them. In the provinces of Collao the huts were made of coarse stones without mortar, and they were about the size and shape of an oven for baking bread. . . . In each one of these huts two Indians always resided. . . . They performed the job of runners or messengers, who with incomparable speed carried the orders and commandments of the Inca to the governors and caciques of the whole kingdom.[98]

The Inca took over many roads from earlier cultures for their own purposes. They established a line of tambos and chasqui stations and distributed their major towns almost equidistantly along the main western highway. They built stone-paved causeways in swampy areas, breached rivers with srope bridges, and maintained a tax system that kept the state fully provisioned. This highly efficient communication and transport system was perhaps the principal reason for their success in incorporating the Collao into their empire, however tenuous that control may have been.

The Inca and the Islands of Lake Titicaca

"On this expedition the Inca subjugated all the towns and nations surrounding the great lake Titicaca . . . along with the islands of the aforesaid lake, which were densely populated at the time."

Bernabé Cobo, *History of the Inca Empire*

The islands in Lake Titicaca were extensively occupied by the time of the Inca Empire. Human use of the major islands goes back to at least 1850 BC, as we learned from an excavation on the Island of the Sun at the site of Ch'uxqullu.[99] Archaeological work on the islands of the Sun and Moon tells us that the Inca intensively occupied both islands, as described below. There was a major Inca settlement on Amantaní Island near the two hills of Pachamama and Pachatata. The entire hillside leading up to the two ceremonial sites was a major Inca village. The sacred court on the hill above the town, known as Pachatata, is clearly built in a pre-Inca style, but it is possible that architectural modifications to the building were made in the Inca period.

Taquile Island has scattered Inca remains, in a pattern similar to that of other large islands in the lake. No systematic work has been conducted on the island, but the Inca occupation was most likely oriented to agricultural production and possibly ritual. At the top of the main hill on the island is a set of Inca-period structures that most likely functioned as storage units. It is possible that these storehouses held maize grown on the island at the time. The island of Tikonata also has Inca remains, as does the neighboring island of Amantaní. On Tikonata, we find numerous finely made Inca objects. Tikonata also grows maize even today, and in the past it was most likely sacred due to this feature. Amantaní is much larger and has many Inca remains. Like Tikonata, maize grows in small sections of the island.

A number of smaller islands in the lake have Inca remains. Isla Quiljata in the south may be representative of these islands. It is a very prominent island, located near the lakeshore in the Chatuma area in the far south of the large lake. The island rises dramatically out of the lake, with very steep sides. Today it is an island, but the lake levels around it are very shallow. In antiquity, and in the recent past, the island was almost certainly connected with the mainland during periods of drought.

Another small island is Pallalla, located northeast of the Island of the Sun. It and Khoa (or Koa) Island are described below.[100] Several islands in Lake Huiñamarca—the little lake—have important Inca remains. There are reports of unique objects found on the island of Pariti. Gregorio Cordero M. published the first account of Inca remains on the islands of Suriki and Intja in Lake Huiñamarca.[101] The Inca walls on Isla Intja, in fact, represent one of the finest examples of Inca architecture in the Titicaca region. Likewise, Estevez and Escalante report on a large Inca occupation on Isla Paco, in the little lake.[102] In this report, they noted massive terrace complexes associated with an Inca occupation. There is also a structure in front of a cut-stone carving in a rock that appears to have been part of an Inca temple complex and pilgrimage destination.

Following page: The Island of Tikonata in the northern Titicaca Basin near Capachica.

169

An Inca Pilgrimage Route to Copacabana and the Islands of the Sun and Moon

One of the most visually beautiful and intellectually fascinating areas of the Titicaca region is the ancient Inca and Tiwanaku sanctuary composed of the towns of Copacabana and Yunguyu, plus the adjacent islands of the Sun and Moon. This pilgrimage destination is located in the far south of Lake Titicaca. The town of Copacabana houses one of the greatest Christian pilgrimage centers in South America: the great church and hilltop shrine with its stations of the cross. The founding of these religious institutions in the Copacabana region is no coincidence. The entire area from Yunguyu on the current Peru–Bolivia border to the Island of the Sun was one large ritual area created by the Inca Empire. Spanish religious authorities unquestionably used the grandeur of this place for their own great church.

The Copacabana complex was one of the most important huacas in the Inca Empire, surpassed only by the Coricancha in the center of Cusco, Paucariqtambo located near Cusco, and possibly Pachacamac on the north-central coast of Peru. This Titicaca basin huaca was actually a series of ancient temples, the largest of which stood beside the sacred Rock of the Sun, a reddish-brown sandstone formation that rises several meters above the land and is located on the far northern end of the island. The finest descriptions of the island come from the priests who lived along the shores of Lake Titicaca during the early seventeenth century. These include the writings of Cobo and the works of two Augustinians: Ramos Gavilán and Fray Antonio de la Calancha.[103]

We can trace the pilgrimage route from Cusco, down the royal road past La Raya, stopping in Hatuncolla and Chucuito, and finally arriving at the first part of the sacred area in Yunguyu. Yunguyu is not coincidentally on the border of Peru and Bolivia, suggesting that this town was on a border region well before Europeans set foot in the area. Pilgrims passed on to Copacabana, making offerings along the way, ultimately arriving at the port of Yampupata. Taking a raft from there, the most likely landing spot on the Island of the Sun was on the far southwestern side of the island.

The first major building is that of Pilco Kayma, located a few hundred meters from the landing spot. Pilco Kayma sits more than 20 meters above the present level of the lake. It has a nearly square main building with some flanking structures and terraces. The site is built in clear Inca-style architecture with some local modifications, particularly diamond-shaped motifs on the terrace walls that are altiplano in style. The extraordinary triple-jamb doorways are hallmarks of Inca canons. Our evidence indicates that the building was once covered with stucco, probably painted with the traditional yellow and red pigments.

Passing to the northeast, the pilgrim would have encountered the Fountain of the Inca, a natural bowl-like area that is extensively terraced and characterized by a series of steps. Curiously, there were no Inca sites found in the entire area flanking the steps. However, there were pre-Inca sites in the area. This may be the source of data in the documents suggesting that the Inca moved indigenous people off the island. It is more likely, given the settlement patterns, that indigenous people were simply moved away from pilgrimage pathways and not off the island itself.

Another important site on the pilgrimage route is Apachinacapata, located on a strategic ridge near the boundary between the modern communities of Yumani and Challa. This site is probably one of the villages mentioned in the chronicles. Apachinacapata has a long cultural history, going back at least 2,000 years before the Inca. There is also a substantial Inca occupation on the site. This large site was a major point in the Inca-period pilgrimage. It is the only site where the two roads intersect, is on the boundary between the communities of Yumani and Challa today, and is a major crossing area. It is precisely for these reasons that the islanders have established a ticket booth here, a custom that definitely goes back to the Inca period.

Another major village along the pilgrimage route was Challapampa. This settlement is located on the isthmus between the main part of the island and the Kalabaya Peninsula. Challapampa is full of Inca pottery on the surface and was probably one of the villages referred to in the chronicles as a way station located several leagues from the Sacred Rock. It was also the home of a hacienda, one of two that controlled the island for centuries, until the land reforms of the 1950s.

The shrine at Copacabana.

Kasapata is located about halfway between Challapampa and the Titikala sanctuary area. It is a major site that covers more than five hectares on an isthmus, again an important pass. The road divides the site almost in half. On the south side of the road is a large Inca structure with five trapezoidal doorways and windows. The building is fairly large for a provincial structure, measuring about 400 square meters. Classic Inca niches were built into the walls. North of the road is a series of stone foundations, terraces, and numerous cut andesite, basalt, and sandstone blocks. Brian Bauer excavated the site. He found carbon on a floor of the building that was early colonial in date. This is very interesting in that the people continued to use this building after the Inca collapse.[104] The nature of that use remains unknown

Opposite: A view of the Copacabana area from the Island of the Sun.

and could range from continued use as a tambo/ritual pilgrimage stop to use as a squatter habitation.

The paved road passes through the wall toward the Sacred Rock. At this point, a series of steps descends to an architectural complex called Mama Ojila. Mama Ojila was described by early chroniclers such as Ramos Gavilán and Cobo and was excavated by Bandelier. There is also a wall around a dry spring that was mentioned by the early Spaniards. The walls of the room on the lower structure align with two islands north of the lake and an intentionally carved cut in the natural ridge to the north. The Proyecto Tiksi Kjarka, which I directed with Brian Bauer, most recently excavated Mama Ojila. This small but important site has three structures, several terrace walls above the road, and a number of smaller walls below. The artifacts and carbon dates confirm the Inca date of the structure. There were very few objects in the buildings themselves, indicating that Mama Ojila was most likely a very sacred spot that was kept clean for special ceremonies.

As early as the sixteenth century, Bernabé Cobo described "footprints of giants" found between Mama Ojila and the Titikala rock. In fact, this is a geological feature typical of this kind of formation, but it indeed does look like a large foot.

The ultimate endpoint of the pilgrimage was the Sacred Rock on the Island of the Sun, known as the Titikala area. The entire sanctuary area is demarcated by a north–south trending fieldstone wall located at the height of the hill overlooking the Sacred Rock area. This, of course, is where the sun was said to have arisen at the beginning of the world. The rock is actually a fairly low sandstone outcrop, with one side sloping toward the lake and the other side rising vertically. A temple was built in the area; it incorporated the natural outcrop to the north and a classic Inca temple wall to the west. The existing temple wall is about 35 meters long. It has a central trapezoidal doorway with a set of eleven small trapezoidal windows. There was probably some kind of construction to the east as well, although most traces of construction have been destroyed. To the west of the Inca wall is a low terraced area. This area contained some structures that were also part of the overall temple complex.

A view of the Copacabana region from Yumani, Island of the Sun.

The historian Bernabé Cobo stresses that the Inca maintained large facilities on the island for the worship of the Sacred Rock. Furthermore, he tells us that this sanctuary was the site of large religious pilgrimages. Because the Island of the Sun was a major center for the Inca, colonists brought in directly from the capital at Cusco kept up the facilities. Cobo says that 2,000 colonists were transported to the island by the Inca. He writes: "[The Inca] brought in other people from Cusco, in whom he could put the trust that the gravity of the case required. He made a moderate-sized town one league from the temple, and the majority of the inhabitants were mitimaes [colonists] of Inca blood and lineage."[105] Ramos Gavilán is even more specific and states that these colonists represented the 42 groups of "Inca by privilege," individuals of some status in the empire who lived in the Cusco region:[106]

Opposite: The ticket booth at Apachinaca, Island of the Sun.

177

"Here [in Copacabana] the Inca transplanted (taking them from their place of birth) Anacuscos, Hurincuscos, Ingas, Chinchaisuyos, Quitos, Pastos, Chachapoyas, Cañares, Cayambis, Latas, Caxamarcas, Guamachucos, Guaylas, Yauyos, Ancaras, Quichuas, Mayos, Guancas, Andesuyos, Condesuyos, Chancas, Aymaras, Ianaguaras, Chumbivilcas, Padrechilques, Collaguas, Hubinas, Canches [Canchis], Canas, Quivarguaros, Lupacas, Capancos, Pucopucos, Pacajes, Iungas, Carangas, Quillacas, Chichas, Soras, Copayapos, Colliyungas, Guánucos, y Huruquillas."[107]

It would therefore appear from the historical documents that the entire peninsula of Copacabana was replaced with colonists from dozens of different ethnic groups from across the empire. The original inhabitants from Copacabana were sent to Yunguyu, the town immediately adjacent to the peninsula on what is now the Peruvian side of the international border. The colonists of Copacabana were responsible for the administration and care of the major temples on the islands of the Sun and Moon, which were dedicated to the glory of the Inca Empire.[108] They may also have been responsible for the cut-stone shrines just outside Copacabana. Several of these groups were from the high-status "Inca by privilege." Additional groups were subject, non-Quechua peoples from the empire.[109] Cobo says there were human and material sacrifices, pilgrimages, and other state-sanctioned ceremonies at these sites.

It is clear that a major pilgrimage route was followed, beginning in Cusco, continuing through to the south Titicaca region via the Urqusuyu road, and ending at the Sacred Rock on the Island of the Sun. Such a long route was not uncommon in ancient states. From the Delian League and Jerusalem in the classical world, through the fragmented states of medieval Christendom in Europe, to the pilgrimages in Hindu and Muslim states, religious and political elites have reworked a particularly "sacred" area into the endpoint of a physical and spiritual journey that transformed a pilgrim from a member of a local ethnic group or village into a participant in a larger state system. The Inca, in fact, were masters of this type of ideological manipulation, drawing on earlier traditions and creating new ones to suit the needs of their empire.

My work with Brian Bauer confirmed the importance of this sacred center to the Inca. As discussed above, work by Matthew Seddon and others also indicates that the islands of the Sun and Moon were used by the earlier Tiwanaku peoples. In fact, they built the original pilgrimage site on the islands. Virtually the entire Island of the Sun was converted into a major ritual landscape during the Tiwanaku and Inca periods. At least two roads, one near the lake and a second on the hill above, reached the northern tip of the island known as the Titikala, or Sacred Rock. The Titikala is a modest, red sandstone outcrop that was considered the origin place of the sun and moon and the place where the founding couple of the Inca dynasty miraculously emerged, according to some of the creation myths described in the classic chronicles.

Excavations by Bauer and his team in front of the Sacred Rock confirmed the use of the area by the Inca, including the use of underground canals to drain liquid offerings at the rock.[110] There were also remains of Inca buildings around and near the rock, all of which generally conformed to historical descriptions by chroniclers such as Cieza de León, Bernabé Cobo, Ramos Gavilán, and Garcilaso de la Vega. Most of these were small hamlets. Others included historically documented sites such as Pilco Kaima, Kasapata, and the Chincana. Still other newly discovered sites included small ceremonial platforms on the hilltops where offerings were left.

The Island of the Sun is a special place. The chroniclers talk about attempts by the Inca to grow coca here. At over 3800 meters above sea level, that would seem impossible. Yet these documents describe a giant hole dug by the Inca to make a warmer microclimate for the sacred plant. Historians record that the hole collapsed and killed the workers and the project was abandoned. Curiously, on the southwestern side of the island there is a microclimate created by the solar radiation and lack of wind. This area is wetter and has some plants, like ferns and braken, that are not found anywhere else on the island. It is posible that this Kona Bay area was where coca was grown. In our research we discovered numerous raised fields and at least one sacred quebrada with Inca architecture. Ancient canals criss-cross the landscape. We also know that the Inca considered the maize grown on the island to be sacred, and taken to Cusco for many ceremonies. In short, Inca use of the

Island of the Sun as a great ceremonial destination for empire-wide pilgrimages was confirmed.

The Sacred Rock Shrine Area and Solstice Worship by the Inca Empire

The marking of the summer and winter solstices was one of the hallmarks of Inca religion. The Inca used stone towers built on hills to mark where the sun rose and set on the December and June solstices. The historian Juan de Betanzos describes the use of these towers in Cusco:

> "So that, as time passed they [the lords of the empire] would not lose count of these months [that the Inca Yupanque created] and the times for sowing and celebrating the fiestas that he had already told them about, he had made those pacha unan chac, which means "clocks." . . . He made the clocks in the following way. Each morning and every afternoon of every month of the year he looked at the sun, watching for the times for sowing and harvesting. Also when the sun went down, he watched the moon when it was new, full, and waning. He had the clocks made of cut stone placed on top of the highest hills at the place where the sun rose and where it went down. . . . Since he could tell the line along which the sun moved as it was setting straight ahead from that place where he stood, he had four marble stone pyramids made on the highest part of the hills. The middle ones were smaller than the ones on the sides. The pyramids [pillars] were two estados high, square and set about one braza apart. . . . As the sun rose, if one stayed where Inca Yupanque stood to look and calculate, the sun comes straight up and goes straight between the pillars, and it did the same when it went down to the place where it sets." [111]

Work on the Island of the Sun also discovered two solstice markers on a hill called Tikani, located above the Sacred Rock. [112] The markers are about a half kilometer northwest of the sacred area (The sacred area is large and imprecisely defined, so a specific distance cannot be provided). As first noted by the archaeoastronomer David Dearborn, the towers mark the winter (June) solstice precisely if one stands in the center of the plaza in the Sacred Rock area.[113] This plaza was demarcated on the northwest by an original wall, to the northeast by the Sacred Rock, and to the southeast by a rise in the landscape. It is not possible to locate the exact sacred area to the southwest, but the topography does not allow much space beyond a few hundred meters in this direction. The towers are very similar to those described in the chronicles for Cusco. They are made of stone and are filled with a solid rubble core. The two towers are about 30 meters apart.

Virtual reality modeling at UCLA indicates that the summer solstice (December) sunset, from the same spot in the temple area where one views the June solstice, falls between the two hills on the nearby island of Chuyu. This island is located to the southwest of the Sacred Rock area.[114] A quick survey of the island did not discover any artifacts on the surface, but the natural hills themselves bracketed

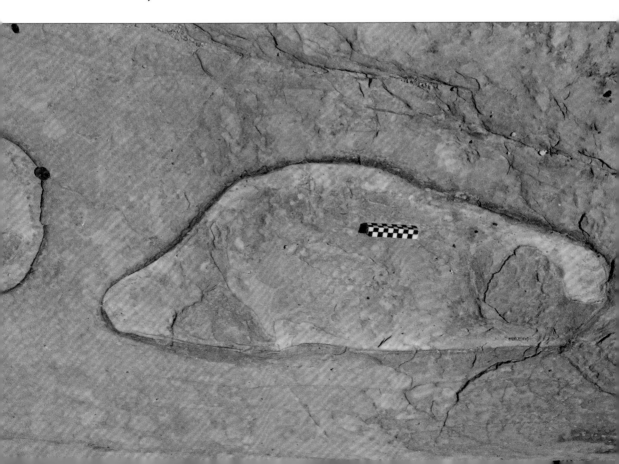

the solstice. It is evident that the December solstice was at least framed by the natural hills on this island, while the Tikani towers framed the June solstice.

Our research also discovered that the solstice ceremonies were more complex than even the historical documents tell us. There was one and only one site that directly abutted the north–south wall above the Titikala that separates the sacred area from the rest of the island. This unnamed site, called by its archaeological registry number 019, is a platform located directly outside the Sacred Rock area. This roughly square platform was first noted by Bandelier.[115] In Bandelier's time, more than 100 years ago, there were actually two "quadrangular" structures at Site 019, suggestive of some kind of duality in the architecture of this sacred spot. The site would have been a slightly elevated area on the low rise between the road and first gate to the sanctuary and the high ground above. The fact that the site was not on the higher area, or adjacent to the road, led Dearborn to check the orientation of the platform relative to the Sacred Rock and the solstice towers. As they explain in their article, Dearborn, Seddon, and Bauer recognized that a person standing in the

middle of this platform would also have a view of the June solstice between the two towers on the Tikani ridge. In fact, the width of the platform (about 30 meters) is similar to the width of the plaza in the Sacred Rock area and the distance between the two towers. Site 019, sitting just outside the sacred area, appears to be the second and only other "special" spot where the solstice can be seen.

The archaeological research conducted by our team allowed us to reconstruct the culmination of a great pilgrimage that Inca peoples made to the Copacabana shrine complex from all over the empire. As one arrives at the first door near Site 019, one has a virtually complete view of the Sacred Rock and the temple complexes. Documents indicate that commoners were not allowed to pass beyond the first gate at the large wall but, as mentioned, were confined to the viewing platform at 019. VIPs and other dignitaries would descend the steps past Mama Ojila onto the main plaza. At this point, the winter solstice ceremony began, marked by the Tikani towers.

The solstice markers on the Island of the Sun functioned almost precisely like those described for Cusco by a number of independent chroniclers. They marked a period of a few days during the winter solstice (June) from the front of the Sacred Rock. There is a special spot in the sacred area, quite near the Sacred Rock, where the sun sets precisely between the two towers. The December (summer) solstice is framed by the hills of Chuyu Island from this spot as well. From this precise location in the Sacred Rock area, the exact date of the June solstice is marked directly in the center of the two towers. As just mentioned, there is a special spot at Site 019 where the sun can be seen to set exactly in the middle of the two towers.

However, there is only one line from which you can see the sun set precisely in the middle of the two towers on this day. That line, of course, goes through the two special spots near the Sacred Rock and on the platform of Site 019. The rest of that sight line would have been either obscured by buildings or off-limits by foot. For instance, a good part of the line between the Sacred Rock and Site 019 is a rocky area that some chronicles state was covered with "gardens." There is, in fact, evidence of springs near Mama Ojila that may have watered these hills. Between the

Summer Solstice
Isla Chuyu
Winter Solstice
Tikani Ridge
Tower
Sac
Murokata
Chucaripupata
Site 019
Upper Road

A view from the high road of the Inca and Tiwanaku sacred zone on the Island of the Sun.

temple area and the Tikani towers, there is some rocky terrain and some low ground. There are no sites or any kind of archaeological remains in this area. In sum, we have no archaeological evidence, either to the northwest or the southeast, of any other platform or building on this sight line.

To repeat, the exact date of the solstice as marked by the Tikani towers can be seen only from two significant spots on the Island of the Sun. The two towers would also have marked about one day before and one day after the precise solstice day from these two spots.[116] In other words, from these two special places, the Inca could mark both a three-day period in which the sun set between the two towers and the precise day of the solstice. In effect, the Tikani towers served to define both a ceremonial period of three days in length and a precise moment when the sun fell exactly between the two towers.

Opposite: Sight lines from the Mama Ojila, Island of the Sun.

From the two special places, one can define the sacred time of the winter solstice ceremony, one that begins with the first sunset through the towers, peaks at the middle sunset, and ends with the last sunset to the other side. The people who were seated or stood in these special places used the towers to define the sacred days. Those days can be precisely fixed, and the precise moment in the middle of that time can be exactly marked. As Dearborn, Seddon, and Bauer note, because the Tikani ridge towers are so close to the Sacred Rock area, the exact spot at which the sun disappears during the solstice "changes visibly as one moves about the plaza." This is an extremely important observation. If we view the towers from another perspective, not as markers of time but as markers of space, we can see why a pair is necessary and how a pair of towers could be used to define sacred space in a place such as the Titikala sanctuary.

As one moves about the Sacred Rock area, in any direction even slightly off the sight line that marks the solstice between the special places and the center of the towers, one has less time to view the setting of the sun during the "official" solstice.

Sight line

Island

Island top

Carved section of natural rock

Wall in site of Mama Ojlia

A map of the Inca sites on the Island of the Sun. Courtesy of A. Vranich.

Of course, the special spots where the solstice sun sets directly in the middle of the two towers determine the "official" time. Dead set in the middle of the plaza on that special spot, or on Site 019 in its special spot, one gets the full three sunsets. These precise spots determine the definition of sacred time. Move a bit to the left or right of that line, and you get less sunset-viewing time. At some point off this line, you cannot see even one day of a sunset during the sacred time as determined by the view of the towers from the special spots.

It is clear how easy it is to mark sacred space at the precise moment of the solstice sunset. At that moment (which lasts for a number of minutes), anybody who can see a sunset through the towers is in the sacred area. If the sun at that moment is blocked by one of the towers, then you are not in the sacred area. Moreover, you

A section of the high road in Challa, in the middle of the Island of the Sun. This is the ancient Inca road to the Sacred Rock.

can see how a cline of sacred space can be constructed. At the first sunset through the towers from the special spots, there will be a well-defined area from which to view the sunset. During the precise moment of the solstice, there will be a slightly different though overlapping area for the sacred space. The same effect would be seen for the third sunset. In other words, people in the special spots will be able to define degrees of sacredness depending on the position of the setting sun. Any spot on the entire landscape of the sacred area can be defined relative to its position to the special spot in the middle. Sacred space is easily defined and understood by all those participating in the ceremonies.

The entire ceremony marked not only the time of the solstices but also the social status of the people participating in the ceremony. One's closeness to the special spots defined one's status in the ritual. Likewise, proximity to the people in the sacred spots corresponded to a person's social status. Like virtually all empires in antiquity, the Inca had a caste structure that defined a person's place in society. As pilgrims participated in the solstice ceremonies, they would be located to greater or lesser degrees near the special spots where the Inca nobility were located. The location of a person in the ceremony at the time of the solstice would be directly correlated to his or her social status. People's entire experience of the solstices would be impacted by where they stood during the sunsets. The closer you were to the highest-ranking person occupying the special spot would determine the degree of status you had at that moment.

It is not, however, a simple correlation of status and distance from the Sacred Rock. We have seen that Site 019 also afforded an unrestricted view of the solstice between the two towers. The location of Site 019 precisely replicates the experience of someone in the sacred area itself in terms of how he or she would witness sunsets during solstice ceremonies. Dearborn, Seddon, and Bauer make a good argument that Site 019 was built for people who were not permitted access to the actual Sacred Rock area. Cobo writes, "[T]hey [common pilgrims] did not get close to the crag

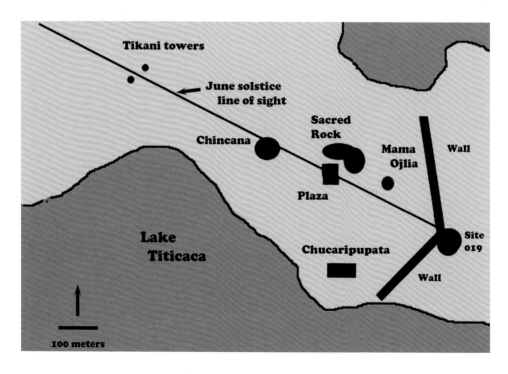

[Sacred Rock]; they were only allowed to view it from the gateway called Intipuncu, and there they handed over their offerings to the attendants who resided there."[117] The Intipuncu was almost certainly the first gate in the wall leading to the Sacred Rock area. The Intipuncu was, in fact, located very close to Site 019. Cobo's reference to pilgrims having to hand their offerings to the guards at the Intipuncu is particularly instructive in this regard. The "special" spot to view the solstice through the Tikani towers was just uphill from the Intipuncu gate, as determined by the archaeological remains.

It can be argued that the people in the special spot at Site 019 actually had substantial status, perhaps even more from their perspective than those in the least-sacred areas of the Sacred Rock sanctuary. In essence, the Inca used the widespread Andean concept of duality to its full expression. They created two roads to the Sacred Rock and created two viewing areas for the June solstice. Even Site 019 had two platforms, perhaps for upper and lower moieties or for people distinguished somehow as uma or urqu. The high road led directly to the Sacred Rock; the lower road led past Site 019 and then onto the Sacred Rock area. We cannot be certain exactly who used the Site 019 platform to view the solstice. What is clear, however, is that the status of the two areas was very complex. There was a hierarchy within the viewing area at Site 019, and this hierarchy was nested within the larger one in the sacred area itself. Politics was complex in the Inca Empire, and the social, political, and even economic ramifications of this great ritual cannot be understated.

An Inca Water Pilgrimage Route?

The existence of a land ritual pilgrimage route from Cusco to the Island of the Sun is little disputed. The route would have followed the Inca road along the western edge of the lake, crossed into the Copacabana Peninsula, and ended up at the origin place of the sun on the Island of the Sun at the Titikala temple. There is some reason to believe that there was a water route as well. In the 1980s, several underwater diving expeditions discovered Inca and Tiwanaku materials on a submerged ridge next to

Opposite: A map of the Sacred Rock area showing the solstice sight lines from the plaza and site 019. Courtesy of A. Vranich.

the island of Khoa, north of the northern part of the Island of the Sun.[118] Johan Reinhard describes a number of ritual objects recovered from the ridge, including cut andesite boxes containing a number of figurines and animal bones, Spondylus shell, gold objects, and pottery. In Reinhard's well-informed opinion, the andesite boxes were of Inca origin and most likely were designed to be lowered onto the underwater ridge. In other words, this particular ridge adjacent to the small island was a place of worship at which objects were intentionally offered in the same way objects were left along land pilgrimage routes.

A number of other islands in the lake have Inca remains and may have been ritually important. Ponce Sangines first reported that the island of Pallalla had prehispanic tombs, most likely based upon information in an early modern document by Joseph Pentland.[119] In our work on the islands of the Sun and Moon sanctuary, we also covered the islands in the immediate vicinity, including Pallalla. On this island, we discovered the foundations of a building about 45 meters long and 6 meters wide, with a series of regularly spaced divisions. The layout is almost certainly that of a colca, or storehouse. Colcas never contain anything these days, because they were used to store items such as cloth and maize. They never stored treasures. So a colca on an island so small suggests a ritual function—a place where pilgrims would stop and rest, perhaps drink chichi, and maybe even sleep. This interpretation is consistent with archaeological data documented by the subaquatic research at Khoa. The alignment of Mama Ojila, described above, also suggests that that particular site was built with at least partial reference to two other islands to the east of the lake.

Certainly, a water pilgrimage route would fit nicely into the uma/urqu (water/land) distinction that was so prominent in Aymara and Quechua cosmology. As mentioned above, the concepts of urqu and uma are well established in the ethnography of the south-central Andes. Urqu refers to land, mountains, and masculinity, while uma refers to water, lowlands, and femininity. The road on the western side of Lake Titicaca was referred to as the Urqusuyu Road, while the one on the east was called Umasuyu.[120] It is quite feasible that the pilgrimage route was also dual in nature—to the west through the Copacabana land route, and through the east on the Umasuyu Road and then to the Island of the Sun by water, with stops on the islands. It is also significant that two roads on the Island of the Sun, one high and one low, led to the Sacred Rock. Such a dual route would parallel in miniature a similar dual route by land and water around the lake as a whole.

The End of Prehistory

In 1534 two of Francisco Pizarro's soldiers were the first Europeans to see the Titicaca region. This great province of the Inca Empire quickly became one of the principal regions in the Spanish Empire of South America. The legacy of Spanish colonization included forced labor in mines, disease, and dislocation. Alongside this exploitation of the native peoples came the construction of magnificent churches throughout the region. The Titicaca area was divided into administrative provinces that shifted through time: the audiencia of Charcas to the south, the viceroyalty of Lima and the viceroyalty of the Río de la Plata as the large divisions, with a number of smaller divisions that somewhat followed indigenous boundaries.

It is ironic that products from the Titicaca area that were so valuable in the prehispanic period—llamas and alpacas, quinoa, fish, and so forth—were replaced with European products such as sheep and goats, wheat, marine fish, and the like. Also, the European obsession with gold and silver and Europe's maritime economy meant that places such as Potosí in the highlands of Bolivia and coastal cities such as Lima were the new focus of human settlement. The Titicaca region during Inca times and before was one of the most accessible places in the Andes, reached by roads that ran up and down the mountains. With the advent of wheeled traffic that isolated the Titicaca region, and the radical shift to a European mercantile economy, the region slipped into a period of decline that continued up to the twentieth century. Fortunately, the emergence of a vigorous tourist economy and the opening of new trade opportunities have led to a resurgence in the economy of the Titicaca region. Not surprisingly, this beautiful and enchanting land is once again flourishing, as it did so often before in its ancient and not-so-ancient past.

Notes

[1] Marion Tschopik, notes on the archaeology of the Department of Puno, 1946, *Papers of the Peabody Museum of American Archaeology and Ethnology*, vol. 27, Harvard University, Cambridge, Massachusetts.

[2] Pedro Cieza de León, chapter 19, in *The Incas of Pedro Cieza de León*, ed. Victor W. von Hagen; trans. Harriet de Onís (1553/1554; reprint, Norman: University of Oklahoma Press, 1976).

[3] Lake Arapa is located in the far northwest. It has a number of bays, such as Puno, Chucuito, and so forth. Lake Huiñamarca, or Lago Menor, is found in the south. Each of these lakes are connected by rivers or narrow straits, and all drain in the south at Desaguadero.

[4] A compromise name that has been suggested is the Islamic Gulf. What this analogy shows us is that there is no "real name" for any lake or other feature shared by different peoples. This was particularly true in the ancient world, where communication was limited.

[5] Ludovico Bertonio, *Vocabulario de la lengua Aymará,* book 2, Juli (1612; facsimile ed., La Paz:, 1956), 353. See also Manuel de Lucca, *Diccionario práctico Aymara-Castellano* (La Paz: Editorial Los Amigos del Libro, 1987).

[6] Weston La Barre, "The Aymara Indians of the Lake Titicaca Plateau, Bolivia," *American Anthropologist* 50, no. 1 (1948): part 2.

[7] Cited in Garcilaso de la Vega, chapter 1, book 3, *The Royal Commentaries of the Inca* (New York: Discus Books, 1961). See also La Barre, "Aymara Indians," 208.

[8] See Garcilaso, *Royal Commentaries*; La Barre, "Aymara Indians," 208; Bertonio, *Vocabulario*, book 2, 389.

[9] Bertonio, *Vocabulario*, book 1, 367; book 2, 343.

[10] Cieza de León, born in Extremadura from a recently converted Jewish family, travelled to the Americas at an early age in the 1530's. He is considered one of the most accurate of the Spanish

Opposite top: the chuch at Tintiri, near Azángaro.
Opposite botton: A beautiful Colonial building in Lampa.
Page 194–195: The beguiling Colonial architecture in Ollantaytambo sits atop an Inca town.

197

chroniclers spending about 16 years visiting and traveling this new land in the European mind. He returned to Spain in 1550 to write his books. His famous *Crónicas* del Perú stands as a classic description of the land and peoples of the western Andes.

11 Most linguists, such as Rodolfo Cerrón-Palomino, argue that the language of the Tiwanaku peoples was Pukina. Most archaeologists see Tiwanaku as a multiethnic and multilingual state that included Aymara-, Pukina-, and Uruquilla-speaking peoples.

12 See David Browman, "Titicaca Basin Archaeolinguistics: Uru, Pukina and Aymara AD 750–1450," *World Archaeology* 26, no. 2 (1994): 235–51.

13 Bertonio, *Vocabulario*, book 1, 288. See also M. J. Hardman-de-Bautista, "Jaqi aru: La lengua humana," in *Raices de America. El mundo Aymara*, ed. Xavier Albó, 155–216 (Madrid: Alianza Editorial, 1988).

14 See Thérèse Bouysse-Cassagne, "Pertenencia étnica, status económico y lenguas en Charcas a fines del siglo XVI," in *Tasa de la visita general de Francisco de Toledo*, ed. David Noble Cook, 312–28 (Lima: Universidad Nacional Mayor de San Marcos, 1975); Alfredo Torero, "Lenguas y pueblos altiplánicos en torno al siglo XVI," *Revista Andina* 5, no. 2 (1987): 329–405; Ruth Shady Solís, "Comments on lenguas y pueblos altiplánicos en torno al siglo XVI by Alfredo Torero," *Revista Andina* 5, no. 2 (1987): 387–92.

15 See Weston La Barre, "The Uru of the Rio Desaguadero," *American Anthropologist* 43, no. 4 (1941): part 1, 493–522.

16 Garci Diez de San Miguel, *Visita hecha a la provincia de Chucuito* (1567; reprint, Lima: Ediciones de la Casa de la Cultura de Perú, 1964), 14.

17 Joyce Marcus, "Prehistoric Fishermen in the Kingdom of Huarco," *American Scientist* 75 (1987): 393–401; María Rostworowski de Diez Canseco, "Guarco y Lunaguaná. Dos señoríos prehispánicos de la costa sur central del Perú," *Revista del Museo Nacional* 44 (1978–80): 153–214.

18 Bertonio, *Vocabulario*, book 2, 380.

19 José Camacho, "Urus, Changos y Atacamas," *Boletín de la sociedad geográfica de La Paz* 66

(1943):9–35; John V. Murra, "Una apreciación etnología de la Visita," in *Visita hecha a la provincia de Chucuito por Garci Diez de San Miguel en el Año 1567* (Lima: Documentos Regionales para el Etnología y Etnohistoria Andinas 1, 1964): 419–444; Thérèse Bouysse-Cassagne, "Tributo y etnias en Charcas en la epoca del Virrey Toledo," *Historia y Cultura 2* (1976): 99; Catherine Julien, *Hatunqolla: A View of Inca Rule from the Lake Titicaca Region,* University of California Publications in Anthropology no. 15 (Berkeley: University of California Press, 1983); Bruce Mannheim, *The Language of the Inka at the Time of Spanish Conquest* (Austin: University of Texas Press, 1991), 50; Torero, Lenguas y pueblos altiplánicos, 332–38; Nathan Wachtel, "Men of the Water: The Uru Problem (Sixteenth and Seventeenth centuries)," in *Anthropological History of Andean Polities*, eds. J. Murra, N. Wachtel, and J. Revel, 283–310 (Cambridge: Cambridge University Press, 1986).

[20] Mannheim, *Language of the Inka*, 50.

[21] Pukina is also referred to by other names, particularly when it is assumed to be an "Uru" language or a variant of Uruquilla. Variant names include Puquina, Poquina, Bokina, Uro, Ochomazo, Uchumi, Kjotsuni, Uroculla, Oroquilla, and Yuracare. See Harriet Manelis de Klein, "Los Urus: el extraño pueblo del altiplano," *Estudios Andinos 7*, vol. 3, no. 1 (1973): 129–50.

[22] Mannheim, *Language of the Inka*, 39.

[23] In 1590 Alonso de Barzana, a Jesuit, wrote a lexicon of Pukina that is now lost, according to Torero, "Lenguas y pueblos altiplánicos," 343.

[24] Following Mannheim, *Language of the Inka*.

[25] e.g., see Torero, "Lenguas y pueblos altiplánicos," and Xavier Albó, "Comments on Lenguas y pueblos altiplánicos en torno al siglo XVI by A. Torero," *Revista Andina 5*, no. 2 (1987): 375–76.

[26] Marion Tschopik, Department of Puno, 566; Adolph Bandelier, *The Islands of Titicaca and Koati* (New York: Hispanic Society of America, 1910), 103; José Huidobro Bellido, Freddy Arce H., and Pascual Quispe Condori, *La verdadera escritura Aymara* (La Paz: Producciones CIMA, 1994), 75.

[27] Cuentas Ormachea, "La danza 'Choqela' y su contenido mágico-religioso," *Boletín de Lima 19* (1982): 54–70.

[28] Occasionally, the yatiri likes to play with the foreign scientist and requests some items that are truly different from most other pagos. The arrival of the naïve foreigner who duly brings the requested objects for is often a source of great amusement for the community.

[29] Joshua and Vera Shapiro, "Lake Titicaca and the House of the Golden Sun Disc," http://members.virtualtourist.com/m/44490/17a761/, accessed January 29, 2010.

[30] Global Oneness, "Sacred Sites: Sacred Waters around the World," http://www.experiencefestival.com/a/Sacred_Sites/id/2321, accessed January 29, 2010.

[31] Ibid.

[32] Brother Philips, *The Secret of the Andes* (London: Neville Spearman, 1961).

[33] George Potter, "Did the Jaredites Land in Peru?" http://64.233.167.104/search?q=cache:yEETQtl06ZEJ:www.nephiproject.com/Newsletter/April%25202007%2520Featured%2520Article.doc+ophir+cieza&hl=en&ct=clnk&cd=4&gl=us, accessed January 29, 2010.

[34] David Hatcher Childress, *Lost Cities and Ancient Mysteries of South America* (Stelle, Ill.: Adventures Unlimited Press, 1986), 244–45.

[35] Peruvian Magic, "Spiritual Journeys 2010," http://www.peruvianmagic.com/spiritual-journeys.html, accessed January 29, 2010.

[36] http://www.spiritjourneys.com/everyone/calendar/peru3dtl.htm, accessed January 29, 2010.

[37] Lost Civilizations, "Inca Ruins," http://www.lost-civilizations.net/inca-ruins-page-3.html, accessed January 29, 2010.

[38] See *International Herald Tribune*, "A Fertility Fable and a Temple to Tourism," March 22, 2006, http://www.iht.com/articles/2006/03/21/features/ruins.php, accessed January 29, 2010.

[39] http://www.freewebs.com/condorspirit/itinerary.htm

[40] Bertonio, *Vocabulario*, book 2, 371.

[41] Sacred Heritage Travel, "Expanded History of Peru," http://www.sacredheritage.com/peru.
expanded.history.html, accessed January 29, 2010.

[42] Aimée Plourde, "*Prestige Goods and Their Role in the Evolution of Social Ranking: A Costly Signaling
Model with Data from the Formative Period of the Northern Lake Titicaca Basin, Peru*" (Ph.D. diss.,
University of California, Los Angeles, 2006).

[43] Amanda Cohen, "*Ritual and Architecture in the Titicaca Basin: The Development of the Sunken Court
Complex in the Formative Period*" (Ph.D. diss., University of California, Los Angeles, 2009).

[44] Robert Feldman, "*Aspero, Peru: Architecture, Subsistence Economy and Other Artifacts of a Preceramic
Maritime Chiefdom*" (Ph.D. diss., Harvard University, 1980); Michael Moseley, *The Incas and Their
Ancestors* (New York: Thames and Hudson, 1992), 120.

[45] Karen Chávez, "The Significance of Chiripa in Lake Titicaca Basin Developments," *Expedition* 30,
no. 3 (1988): 17–26.

[46] Sergio Chávez, "*The Conventionalized Rules in Pucara Pottery Technology and Iconography: Implications
for Socio-Political Developments in the Northern Lake Titicaca Basin*" (Ph.D. diss., Michigan State
University, Lansing, 1992); Elizabeth Klarich, "*From the Monumental to the Mundane: Defining Early
Leadership Strategies at Late Formative Pukara, Peru*" (Ph.D. diss., University of California, Santa Barbara,
2005).

[47] The site was excavated by several noted early archaeologists, including Gregorio Cordero,
Alfred Kidder II, and others. Later, the work of David Browman and Karen Chávez helped us
understand the nature of the site even more. Most recently, the work of Christine Hastorf and her
team has revealed countless secrets of this lost civilization. See Christine Hastorf, "Community
with the Ancestors: Ceremonies and Social Memory in the Middle Formative at Chiripa, Bolivia,"
Journal of Anthropological Archaeology 22, no. 4 (2003): 305–32.

[48] William Conklin and Michael Moseley, "The Patterns of Art and Power in the Early
Intermediate Period," in *Peruvian Prehistory*, ed. Richard Keatinge, 145-163. (New York: Cambridge
University Press, 1988).

49 We are able to determine this through archaeological surveys. Surveys are conducted by one or two crews of four or five archaeologists each. The survey team walks the entire landscape, finding and recording sites. Collections of pottery and stone tools from the surface allow us to determine the ages of the various sites and provide a broad picture of the historical trajectory over many centuries or millennia.

50 See Alan Kolata and Carlos Ponce Sanjines, "Tiwanaku: The City at the Center," in *The Ancient Americas,* ed. Richard Townsend, 317–33 (Chicago: Art Institute of Chicago, 1992); Juan Albarracin-Jordan and James Edward Mathews, *Asentamientos prehispánicos del valle de Tiwanaku,* vol. 1 (La Paz: Producciones CIMA, 1990); Juan Albarracin-Jordan, Tiwanaku. *Arqueología regional y dinámica segmentaria* (La Paz: Editores Plural, 1996); Linda Manzanilla, *Akapana. Una pirámide en el centro del mundo* (Mexico City: UNAM, 1992); Javier F. Escalante Moscoso, *Arquitectura prehispánica en los Andes Bolivianos* (La Paz: Produccion Cima, 1994).

51 This paragraph uses information described in John Wayne Janusek, *Identity and Power in the Ancient Andes: Tiwanaku Cities through Time* (New York: Routledge, 2004).

52 Sergio J. Chávez and Karen L. Mohr-Chávez, "A Carved Stela from Taraco, Puno, Peru and the Definition of an Early Style of Stone Sculpture from the Altiplano of Peru and Bolivia," *Nawpa Pacha* 13 (1975): 45–83; Alan Kolata, *The Tiwanaku* (London: Blackwell, 1993), 141–42; Michael Moseley, "Structure and History in the Dynastic Lore of Chimor," in *The Northern Dynasties: Kingship and Statecraft in Chimor,* eds. M. Moseley and A. Cordy-Collins, 1–41 (Washington, D.C.: Dumbarton Oaks, 1990).

53 Sergio Chávez, "La piedra del rayo y la estela de Arapa: un caso de identidad estilística, Pucara-Tiahuanaco," *Arte y Arqueología* 8–9 (1984): 1–27.

54 Ronald McNair Scott, *Robert the Bruce, King of Scots* (New York: Peter Bedrick Books, 1989) 37.

55 Kolata, *Tiwanaku.*

56 John Janusek, *Ancient Tiwanaku* (New York: Cambridge University Press, 2008), 145.

57 Carlos Ponce, *Tiwanaku: 200 años de investigaciones arqueológicas* (La Paz: CIMA, 1995) 243·

58 J.P. Protzen and Stella Nair, "The Gateways of Tiwanaku: Symbols or Passages? in *Andean Archaeology II: Art, Landscape, and Society,* eds. H. Silverman and W. H. Isbell, 189–223 (New York: Kluwer Academic Publishers, 2002).

59 Brian Bauer and Charles Stanish, *Ritual and Pilgrimage in the Ancient Andes* (Austin: University of Texas Press, 2001); Charles Stanish and Brian Bauer, *Archaeological Research on the Islands of the Sun and Moon, Lake Titicaca, Bolivia: Final Results from the Proyecto Tiksi Kjarka* (Los Angeles: Cotsen Institute of Archaeology, UCLA, 2004).

60 Matthew Thomas Seddon, *"Excavations in the Raised Fields of the Río Catari Sub-Basin, Bolivia"* (Master's thesis, University of Chicago, 1994).

61 Adolph Bandelier, *The Islands of Titicaca and Koati* (New York: Hispanic Society of America, 1910). Bandelier is one of the most enigmatic figures in early archaeology in the Americas. He was well known as a scholar who traveled and worked the extent of the Americas and is credited with many important scholarly findings. On the other hand, he did not interact well with the Aymara peoples of the Island of the Sun, who reciprocated the negative feelings they felt from him by leading Bandelier astray on numerous occasions while he tried to do his work. See Charles Stanish, *Ancient Titicaca* (Berkeley: University of California Press, 2003).

62 Marc Bermann, Paul Goldstein, Charles Stanish, and Luis Watanabe, "The Collapse of the Tiwanaku State: A View from the Osmore Drainage," in *Ecology, Settlement and History in the Osmore Drainage*, eds. D. Rice, C. Stanish, and P. Scarr, 269–86 (Oxford: British Archaeological Reports, 1989).

63 Paul Goldstein, "Tiwanaku Temples and State Expansion: A Tiwanaku Sunken Court Temple in Moquegua, Peru," *Latin American Antiquity* 4, no. 3 (1993): 22–47.

64 Michael E. Moseley, Donna J. Nash, Patrick R. Williams, Susan D. deFrance, Ana Miranda and Mario Ruales, "Burning Down the Brewery: Establishing and Evacuating an Ancient Imperial Colony at Cerro Baúl, Peru," *Proceedings of the National Academy of Sciences*, (2005):102:17264-17271.

65 Charles R. Ortloff and Alan L. Kolata, "Climate and Collapse: Agro-ecological Perspectives on the Decline of the Tiwanaku State," *Journal of Archaeological Science* 20 (1993): 195–221.

66 Alan Kolata, "The Agricultural Foundations of the Tiwanaku State: A View from the Heartland," *American Antiquity* 51, no. 4 (1986): 748–62.

67 Michael Binford and Mark Brenner, "Resultados de estudios de limnología en los ecosistemas de Tiwanaku," in *Arqueología de Lukurmata*, ed. Alan Kolata, 213–36 (La Paz: Producciones Pumapunku, 1989); Michael Binford, Mark Brenner, and D. Engstrom, "Patrones de sedimentación temporal en la zona litoral del Huiñaimarca," in *El Lago Titicaca: síntesis del conocimiento*, eds. C. DeJoux and A. Iltis, 47–58 (La Paz: ORSTROM/HISBOL, 1992); Michael Binford, Mark Brenner, and Barbara Leyden, "Paleoecology and Tiwanaku Ecosystems," in *Tiwanaku and Its Hinterland: Archaeology and Paleoecology of an Andean Civilization*, ed. Alan Kolata, 90–108 (Washington, D.C.,: Smithsonian Institution, 1996).

68 Cieza de León, *Incas*, ch. 100.

69 See Escalante Moscoso, Arquitectura prehispánica, 329; Bouysse-Cassagne, "Urco and Uma: Aymara Concepts of Space," in *Anthropological History of Andean Polities*, eds. John Murra, Norman Wachtel and Jacques Revel, 201-227 (Cambridge: Cambridge University Press, 1986)

70 This map is adapted from several sources, including Bouysse-Cassagne, "Pertenencia étnica"; Julien, *Hatunqolla*; and Torero, "Lenguas y pueblos altiplánicos."

71 See Julien, *Hatuncolla*.

72 Kolata, *The Tiwanaku*.

73 Bertonio *Vocabulario*, book 2, 239, 374; Bouysse-Cassagne, "Urco and Uma," 202; Kolata, *The Tiwanaku*, 8.

74 Bouysse-Cassagne, "Urco and Uma," 209; Kolata, *The Tiwanaku*, 8–9.

75 Cieza de León, *Incas*, ch. 100.

76 Fernando de Montesinos, *Anales del Perú* (1642; reprint, Madrid: Editorial de Víctor Maúrtua, 1906).

[77] Bernabé Cobo, *History of the Inca Empire*, trans. Roland Hamilton (1653; reprint, Austin: University of Texas Press, 1979), 140.

[78] I thank Lawrence Keeley for information regarding this fortification technique.

[79] John Hyslop, "*An Archaeological Investigation of the Lupaca Kingdom and Its Origins*" (Ph.D. diss., Columbia University, New York, 1976).

[80] There is no direct evidence of Lupaqa chulpas at Sillustani. The styles of the chulpas and the great variety of chulpa types suggest that all groups in the region indeed did have a presence at Sillustani. Most compelling, however, is the theoretical understanding that such pilgrimage destinations tend to be used by many peoples as "neutral" places, where many groups come together. Even enemies are rarely engaged in continuous conflict. During the expectedly long periods of truce between enemies, it is likely that such destinations were used by all peoples in the region in a manner similar to Delphi in central Greece, where many polities maintained temples and installations for periodic panregional feasts and events when a general peace prevailed.

[81] Rosanna Liliana Revilla Becerra and Mauro Alberto Uriarte Paniagua, "*Investigación arqueológica en la zona de Sillustani-Sector Wakakancha-Puno*" (Bachelor's thesis, Universidad Católica Santa María, 1985).

[82] Edmundo de la Vega and Charles Stanish, "Los centros de peregrinaje como mecanismos de integración política en sociedades complejas del altiplano del Titicaca," *Boletín de Arqueología PUCP* 6 (2002): 265–275.

[83] See Bauer and Stanish, *Ritual and Pilgrimage*, for a discussion of Island of the Sun data.

[84] Catherine Julien, "Inca Decimal Administration in the Lake Titicaca Region, in *The Inca and Aztec States, 1400–1800: Anthropology and History*, eds. G. Collier, R. Rosaldo, and J. Wirth, 119–55 (New York: Academic Press, 1982).

[85] Cieza de León, *Incas*, ch. 102.

[86] For more information on Hatuncolla, see Julien, Hatunqolla, 89.

[87] Brian Bauer, personal communication, 1994.

[88] There are some "phallic-shaped" cut stones in the Inca Uyu. Most of the smaller stones are probably authentic and were used in agricultural constructions as steps (as seen in famous Inca terracing at Pisac and Raqchi). However, the more "elaborate" stones are probably not aboriginal but apparently were commissioned by a collector and assembled in the Inca Uyu sometime in the twentieth century. They have since become a New Age phenomenon on the tourist circuit, with inaccurate but humorous interpretations of sacred mushrooms, fertility symbols, and the like.

[89] See María Rostworowski's excellent *History of the Inca Realm* (Cambridge: Cambridge University Press, 1999).

[90] The numbers of warriors are from Cieza de León and are almost certainly exaggerated.

[91] Catherine Julien, "A Late Burial from Cerro Azoguini, Puno," *Nawpa Pacha* 19 (1981): 144.

[92] See the *Toledo Tasa* in Cook, Francisco de Toledo, 59.

[93] John Hyslop, *The Inka Road System* (New York: Academic Press, 1984).

[94] Katharina Schreiber, "Conquest and Consolidation: A Comparison of the Wari and Inka Occupations of a Highland Peruvian Valley, *American Antiquity* 52, no. 2 (1987): 266–84.

[95] Ephraim Squier, *Incidents of Travel and Exploration in the Land of the Incas* (New York: Harper and Brothers, 1877).

[96] Julien, *Hatunqolla*, 24.

97 Hyslop, *Inka Road System·*

98 Bernabé Cobo, *History of the Inca Empire;* Bernabé Cobo, *Inca Religion and Customs* (1653; reprint, Austin: University of Texas Press, 1990).

99 Charles Stanish, Richard Burger, Lisa Cipolla, Michael Glascock, and Esteban Quelima, "Evidence for Early Long-Distance Obsidian Exchange and Watercraft Use from the Southern Lake Titicaca Basin of Bolivia and Peru," *Latin American Antiquity* 13, no. 4 (2002): 444–54.

100 Carlos Ponce Sanginés, Johan Reinhard, Max Portugal, Eduardo Pareja, and Leocadio Ticlla, *Exploraciones arqueológicas subacuáticas en el Lago Titikaka* (La Paz: Editorial La Palabra, Producciones, 1992).

101 Gregorio Cordero Miranda, "Estudio preliminar en las islas de Intja and Suriki del Lago Titikaka," *Pumapunku* 5 (1972): 22–39.

102 José Estéves Castillo and Javier Escalante Moscoso, *Investigaciónes arqueológicas in la Isla Pako (a Suriqui)* (La Paz: Documentos Internos INAR, 1994).

103 Cobo, *History of the Inca Empire; Inca Religion and Customs*; Alonso Ramos Gavilán, *Historia del santuario de Nuestra Señora de Copacabana* (1621; reprint, Lima: Ignacio Prado P., 1988); Antonio de la Calancha, *Corónica moralizada del orden de San Augustín en el Perú,* ed. I. Prado Pastor, (1638; reprint, Lima,1981).

104 Bauer and Stanish, *Ritual and Pilgrimage*, 178.

105 Cobo, *History of the Inca Empire; Inca Religion and Customs*, book 13, ch. 18.

106 Ramos Gavilán, *Historia del santuario*, ch. 12.

107 Ibid., 84–85.

108 Julien, *Hatunqolla*, 88.

109 Brian Bauer, *The Development of the Inca State* (Austin: University of Texas Press, 1992).

110 Brian S. Bauer, Mary Futrell, Lisa Cipolla, R. Alan Covey, and Joshua Terry, "Excavations at Inca Sites on the Island of the Sun," in *Archaeological Research on the Islands of the Sun and Moon, Lake Titicaca, Bolivia: Final results of the Proyecto Tiksi Kjarka,* eds. Charles Stanish and Brian S. Bauer, (Los Angeles: Cotsen Institute of Archaeology, UCLA, 2004).

111 Juan de Betanzos, *Narrative of the Incas*, trans. and eds. Roland Hamilton and Dana Buchanan (1557; reprint, Austin: University of Texas Press, 1996).

112 The scientific process that led to the discovery of the towers was quite interesting. They were first discovered on survey by the author and listed as burial towers or chulpas. After the survey, archaeoastronomer David Dearborn and Inca specialist Brian Bauer noted that the towers were in the general direction of the winter solstice. Later archaeoastronomical work and excavations by Dearborn, Mathew Seddon, and Bauer definitely proved that these were indeed solid, rubble-filled towers and not burials. For technical descriptions of the towers, see Matthew Seddon and Brian Bauer, "Excavations at Tikani," in *Archaeological Research on the Islands of the Sun and Moon, Lake Titicaca, Bolivia: Final Results of the Proyecto Tiksi Kjarka,* eds. Charles Stanish and Brian S. Bauer, (Los Angeles: Cotsen Institute of Archaeology, UCLA, 2004).

113 Published in David Dearborn, Matthew Seddon, and Brian Bauer, "The Sanctuary of Titicaca,

Where the Sun Returns to Earth," *Latin American Antiquity* 9, no. 3 (1998): 240–58.

114 The modeling was conducted by the UCLA Virtual Reality Laboratory and funded by a grant to Barnard Frischer and the author by Verizon/GTE. Additional funding was graciously provided by Charles Steinmetz and the Steinmetz Family Foundation. Dean Abernathy wrote the model. I thank all involved for providing us these resources.

115 See Bauer and Stanish, *Ritual and Pilgrimage*, 180.

116 Brian Bauer, personal communication, 2006.

117 Cobo, *Inca Religion and Customs*, 96.

118 Ponce et al., *Exploraciones arqueológicas subacuáticas* 1992; and see Johan Reinhard, "High Altitude Archaeology and Mountain Worship in the Andes," *American Alpine Journal* 25 (1983): 54–67.

119 Joseph Barclay Pentland, *Informe sobre Bolivia* (1826), trans. Jack Aitken Soux (Potosi, Bolivia: Editorial Potosi, 1975).

120 Hyslop, *The Inka Road System,* 263–64.

Glossary

altiplano: The high plains of the central and southern Andes, characterized by vast grasslands and rolling hills.

ayllu: A social unit of related people who hold land and other resources.

cabecera: A central political or administrative town in any region.

Canas: An ethnic group found on the Cusco side of the La Raya Pass.

Canchis: An ethnic group found on the Cusco side of the La Raya Pass.

Cari: A king of the Lupaqa people in the late prehistoric and early historic period of the Lake Titicaca region.

chasqui: A runner or messenger in the Inca Empire who delivered instructions or carried light objects for the royal authorities.

Choquela: A social designation for people who lived in the remote areas of the Titicaca region, outside the reach of political authorities. The term also refers to a ritual dance involving vicuña hunting.

Chucuito: The capital of the Lupaqa kingdom, found in the city of the same name, a few kilometers north of Puno.

chulpa: An aboveground burial tower found in the central and southern Andes.

colca: An Inca storage building, usually found at administrative centers and along the road system.

Colla: An Aymara-speaking ethnic group in the northwestern and northern Titicaca region of the late prehistoric and early historic period.

Collao: A general term for the Titicaca region in the early historic period.

Collasuyu: The Inca name for the province of the Titicaca region.

Hatuncolla: The capital of the Colla kingdom, found in the city of the same name, a few kilometers southeast of Sillustani.

huaca: A sacred place or object that represented the essence of a people, village, clan, or other group.

kalasasaya: An enclosure, usually of stone, that was associated with pyramids and sunken courts. The Kalasasaya is the name of the great enclosure at the site of Tiwanaku.

kenko: A carved natural rock formation used for rituals in the Inca Empire.

Lupaqa: An Aymara-speaking ethnic group in the western Titicaca region of the late prehistoric and early historic period.

mitimaes: Colonists transplanted by the Inca state for strategic and economic purposes.

Moquegua: A valley on the Pacific watershed, about 100 kilometers west of Lake Titicaca.

Omasuyus: The region east of Lake Titicaca that included the lakeshore and the Amazonian watershed.

Pacajes: The region and people of the south Titicaca area. Pacajes was the ancestral home of the Tiwanaku kingdom.

pago: A "payment" to the earth or the gods conducted by religious specialists.

Pucara: A major town, archaeological site, and culture in the northern Titicaca region.

pukara: A term that means "fortress" in Aymara and Quechua.

Quelccaya: A glacier in the central Andes studied for the reconstruction of ancient climate.

Sillustani: A major site and pilgrimage destination in the late prehistoric period in the northwestern Titicaca region.

Spondylus. A bivalve mollusk also known as Pacific thorny oyster (Spondylus princeps) that was considered a luxury good in the Prehispanic Andes.

tambo: A way station or storage building located on Inca highways.

Tiwanaku: The site and culture of the great kingdom of the first millennium AD, located in the town and valley of the same name in Bolivia.

taypi: An Aymara concept that means "middle" or "center".

tinku: A form of ritualized battle common in the central Andes.

Titikala: The sandstone rock on the Island of the Sun that was sacred to the Inca and where the sun and moon rose in their religion.

urcu: The concept of earth, mountains, and so forth that is paired with the complementary concept of uma.

ushnu: An Inca ritual platform.

Uru: An ethnic people in the Titicaca region who live on artificial floating islands.

yatiri: A religious specialist or expert in Aymara society.

Zapana: A king of the Colla, a late prehistoric and early historic kingdom in the northwestern Titicaca area.

Index